Language in Education:
Theory and Practice

FOREIGN LANGUAGE in the ELEMENTARY SCHOOL: STATE of the ART

FOREIGN LANGUAGE in the ELEMENTARY SCHOOL: STATE of the ART

by Linda Schinke-Llano

A publication of **CAL** Center for Applied Linguistics

Prepared by **ERIC** Clearinghouse on Languages and Linguistics

HBJ HARCOURT BRACE JOVANOVICH, INC.

Orlando   San Diego   New York   Toronto   London   Sydney   Tokyo

LANGUAGE IN EDUCATION: Theory and Practice 62

 This publication was prepared with funding
from the National Institute of Education,
U.S. Department of Education under contract
no. 400-82-009. The opinions expressed in
this report do not necessarily reflect the
positions or policies of NIE or ED.

Printed in the United States

ISBN 0-15-599314-3

Language in Education: Theory and Practice

ERIC (Educational Resources Information Center) is a nationwide network of information centers, each responsible for a given educational level or field of study. ERIC is supported by the National Institute of Education of the U.S. Department of Education. The basic objective of ERIC is to make current developments in educational research, instruction, and personnel preparation more readily accessible to educators and members of related professions.

ERIC/CLL. The ERIC Clearinghouse on Languages and Linguistics (ERIC/CLL), one of the specialized clearinghouses in the ERIC system, is operated by the Center for Applied Linguistics. ERIC/CLL is specifically responsible for the collection and dissemination of information in the general area of research and application in languages, linguistics, and language teaching and learning.

LANGUAGE IN EDUCATION: THEORY AND PRACTICE. In addition to processing information, ERIC/CLL is also involved in information synthesis and analysis. The Clearinghouse commissions recognized authorities in languages and linguistics to write analyses of the current issues in their areas of specialty. The resultant documents, intended for use by educators and researchers, are published under the title Language in Education: Theory and Practice. The series includes practical guides for classroom teachers and extensive state-of-the-art papers.

This publication may be purchased directly from the
Center for Applied Linguistics. It also will be
announced in the ERIC monthly abstract journal
Resources in Education (RIE) and will be available
from the ERIC Document Reproduction Service,
Computer Microfilm International Corp., P.O. Box
190, Arlington, VA 22210. See RIE for ordering
information and ED number.

For further information on the ERIC system,
ERIC/CLL, and Center/Clearinghouse publications,
write to ERIC Clearinghouse on Languages and
Linguistics, Center for Applied Linguistics, 1118
22nd St., N.W., Washington, D.C. 20037.

Gina Doggett, editor, Language in Education

Acknowledgments

I would like to express my appreciation to Gina
Doggett and Nancy Rhodes for their unflagging patience
and support; to Emily Murphy and Adrienne Cannon for
compiling the bibliography; to Mary O'Rourke, Diane
James, and Rebecca Blattner for their diligent typing;
and, most importantly, to Frank and Melissa, without
whose cooperation such projects could never be undertaken.

Linda Schinke-Llano
Evanston, Illinois

Preface

This monograph discusses the state of the art of foreign language instruction in the elementary schools in the United States. It explores the past and the present, the successes and the failures, the ideal and the actual, and the theoretical and the practical.

Chapter 1 presents the various types of early foreign language programs that have been implemented. Foreign language experience (FLEX) programs, foreign language in the elementary school (FLES) programs, and immersion models are discussed with respect to goals, the degree of integration with the total curriculum, and the roles played by English and the foreign language.

Chapter 2 provides the rationale for early foreign language study. Two perspectives are represented: that of the first wave of early foreign language programs in the 1950s and '60s, and that of the current wave in the '80s. Whereas the former perspective is best categorized by the motto "the earlier the better," the current perspective acknowledges both advantages and disadvantages in early foreign language learning.

Chapter 3 discusses research evidence concerning the effectiveness of early foreign language programs. This evidence is viewed in light of current second language acquisition theory, and suggestions for future research topics are made.

Chapter 4 is devoted to the procedures involved in the implementation of an early foreign language program. Essential steps are outlined, from the establishment of a steering committee to the formulation of evaluation procedures.

Since evaluation is an essential component of any early foreign language program, Chapter 5 continues with a more detailed discussion of evaluation issues. Basic concepts in evaluation design are presented, as well as an outline of procedures to be followed in the evaluation process.

Because any state-of-the-art discussion runs the risk of becoming obsolete almost immediately, Chapter 6 suggests areas in early foreign language education that are in need of development. Highlighted are the need for the development of adequate language assessment tools, the establishment of an informational clearinghouse, a systematic public relations effort, and, of course, continued research.

A bibliography and resource information appear in Chapter 7.

Contents

Because of the enrichment nature of FLEX programs, they are decidedly viewed as supplementary to the basic elementary school curriculum. Foreign language experience classes may meet during the school day, but quite often they are held before or after regularly scheduled classes. In addition, as compared with the other early foreign language programs, FLEX classes meet relatively less frequently and for relatively shorter periods of time. For example, classes in a FLEX program may meet once or twice a week for 20 or 30 minutes each time. Aside from the efforts of individual teachers to relate the content of FLEX classes to that of other school subjects, there is often no concerted effort to integrate a FLEX program into the total school curriculum. However, some schools with FLEX programs do take a more global approach to all their subjects.

Given the limited goals and the supplementary nature of a FLEX program, the foreign language being studied is used relatively little in the classroom. In a U.S. setting, for example, English is usually the medium of instruction, with the foreign language serving as the target of instruction. That is, English is used to "talk about" French or Spanish or German, for example. It is precisely this limited use of the foreign language that makes FLEX programs attractive to a district that wishes to implement early foreign language programs. Because English may be used as the medium of instruction, foreign language specialists need not be hired. With very basic training, and self-explanatory audiotapes, teachers with no prior background can develop appropriate language and cultural enrichment activities for their students (Rhodes, 1981).

Foreign Language in the Elementary School

Introduced in the 1950s, foreign language in the elementary school (FLES) programs enjoyed a heightened period of popularity during the 1960s. Now, after more than a decade of inactivity, "revitalized" FLES programs have begun to appear in U.S. public schools. Children in these programs are expected to (a) acquire a degree of proficiency in listening and speaking, (b) develop cultural awareness, and (c) attain some degree of proficiency in reading and writing (Gray, Rhodes, Campbell, & Snow, 1984). Of course, the desired levels of proficiency in the four skill areas of listening, speaking, reading, and writing vary from program to program. In all instances, however, the goals of FLES programs are more ambitious than FLEX programs with respect to anticipated levels of language proficiency.

FLES programs may be regarded as enrichment programs, or as an integral part of the academic curriculum. Depending on the school district, FLES classes may be scheduled before, during, or after the academic day. Generally, FLES programs provide foreign language instruction three to five days a week, for a total of two to five hours of weekly instruction (Gray, Rhodes, Campbell, & Snow, 1984). As in the case of schools with FLEX programs, individual teachers in FLES schools may attempt to relate the activities in the foreign language class to those in other content areas.

With respect to the roles played by English and the foreign language, FLES programs are both similar to and distinct from FLEX programs. Both programs often use English as the medium of instruction, with the foreign language functioning as the target of instruction. However, since FLES programs emphasize the attainment of a certain level of oral proficiency rather than the ability to recognize a limited vocabulary, a larger portion of class time is devoted to the use of the foreign language, and often the class is conducted solely in the foreign language. Given this need for greater use of the foreign language, school districts generally hire a foreign language specialist or reassign a teacher with the desired foreign language skills.

A type of FLES program that is an integral part of the academic curriculum is sometimes referred to as "curriculum-integrated." A relatively recent addition to early foreign language education, the curriculum-integrated foreign language program conducts daily foreign language classes and includes additional language and culture instruction taught by the regular

classroom teacher. It seeks to develop the four skill areas of listening, speaking, reading, and writing to higher levels of proficiency than those intended in FLES programs, which are more conversation oriented.

The distinctive nature of the curriculum-integrated program is further exemplified by the roles played by English and the foreign language. Unlike FLEX and some FLES classes, language classes in this model are conducted in the foreign language itself. Thus, the foreign language serves as both the medium and target of instruction. English, if used at all in the language class, is reserved for the purpose of clarifying information. The additional language and cultural information, provided by the classroom teacher during another part of the day, may be presented in English. It is precisely this use of the foreign language as a medium of instruction that fosters the development of the higher levels of proficiency that are desired.

Immersion

Unlike FLEX and FLES programs, language immersion programs are distinguished by the use of the foreign language as the medium of instruction for content area subjects. The first language immersion program in North America was established in 1965 in the Montreal suburb of St. Lambert (Lambert & Tucker, 1972). Influenced by the success of this and subsequent immersion programs in Canada, public school officials in Culver City, CA, in conjunction with scholars at UCLA, replicated the St. Lambert model in 1971 (Campbell, 1972, 1984). Since then, at least 17 other school districts in the United States have established programs (Rhodes, personal communication, December 1984). In virtually all cases, immersion programs have four specified goals: foreign language fluency, continued development of English, subject matter achievement, and appreciation of the foreign culture and its representatives (Campbell, 1984; Lambert & Tucker, 1972). Further, proficiency in listening, speaking, reading, and writing is stressed in both English and the foreign language.

Chapter 1
Early Foreign Language Study

PROGRAM TYPES

As a prerequisite for examining the status of foreign language instruction in the elementary schools in the United States, it is essential to identify the variety of program types being implemented. At present, three basic programmatic approaches exist: FLEX, FLES, and immersion. Each type of program may be distinguished by its goals, which state both the level of fluency and the number of skills to be developed; the level of integration with the total curriculum that is desired; and the roles that English and the foreign language are expected to play.

Foreign Language Experience

Foreign language experience (FLEX) programs were begun in the 1970s in response to increased interest in foreign languages, as well as to decreased funding for special programs. The goal of FLEX programs is to provide children with exposure to a foreign language and culture, not to develop fluency (Rhodes & Schreibstein, 1983). Generally, only oral skills are highlighted, with the content of FLEX classes focusing on the development of vocabulary (such as numbers, colors, and days of the week) and cultural knowledge (via ethnic food, music, and costumes). On occasion, up to three languages may be introduced in this manner during a single academic year.

Thus, language immersion programs are an integral part of the school curriculum. Immersion programs do, however, differ in the nature of their integration with the total academic program. Immersion programs may be classified according to the "degree of immersion," the grade level at which they are implemented, and the number of target languages included (Schinke-Llano, 1984).

With respect to the degree of immersion, programs are classified as either total or partial. In total immersion programs, the foreign, or target, language is used for the entire curriculum at the outset (Genesee, 1984; Lapkin & Cummins, 1984). English is introduced into the curriculum after a period of time, generally after two, three, or even four years of participation in the program (Genesee, 1978b; Genesee & Lambert, 1983; Lambert & Tucker, 1972). Once English is included in the program, its use as a medium of instruction may vary from 20 percent of the time (Morrison, Bonyun, Pawley, & Walsh, 1979) to 60 percent (Genesee, 1978b), depending on the individual program or the particular grade level within a program. Partial immersion, on the other hand, is characterized by use of the foreign language for less than 100 percent of the curriculum at the outset of the program. Generally the foreign language is used half the time, with decreases in usage, if any, occurring after a number of years (Genesee, 1984; Lapkin & Cummins, 1984).

With respect to the grade level of implementation, immersion programs are designated as early, delayed, or late (Genesee, 1984; Lapkin & Cummins, 1984). Early immersion begins in kindergarten or first grade. In delayed immersion programs, the foreign language is introduced as a medium of instruction in the fourth or fifth grade. In late immersion programs, use of the foreign language to teach content subjects is not begun until late in the elementary school years, or even early in the secondary school years. Both delayed and late programs may be preceded by one or several years of traditional foreign language instruction, that is, classes in which the foreign language is the target of instruction.

The grade level of implementation of an immersion

program determines, among other things, one very important aspect of a child's education, namely the language in which literacy skills are initiated. In an early total immersion program, for example, literacy training is begun in the foreign language; in an early partial program, literacy is often developed simultaneously in English and the foreign language. Before beginning delayed and late programs, on the other hand, students have acquired literacy skills in English, that is, their native language.

Regarding the number of target languages included in the curriculum, programs may provide either single or double immersion. This designation obviously counts the number of foreign languages used for instructional purposes. Hypothetically, of course, triple and quadruple immersion programs could exist.

Theoretically, many combinations of the program types discussed are possible (e.g., early partial single immersion, delayed total double immersion). In actuality, single immersion programs predominate. While early programs are either total or partial, there is a tendency for delayed and late programs to be partial (Genesee, 1984; Lapkin & Cummins, 1984).

Regardless, however, of the degree of immersion, the grade level of implementation, or the number of target languages involved, all immersion programs have one essential characteristic: The foreign language is used not only as the target of instruction, but also, and more importantly, as the medium of instruction in subject matter classes. It is precisely this broader use of the foreign language--in communicative contexts similar to those in which a first language is acquired--that immersion proponents say facilitates the acquisition of a second language.

SUMMARY

Existing foreign language programs in the elementary school may be distinguished according to three basic approaches: FLEX, FLES, and immersion. Each program type is identifiable by its goals, the extent of integration with the total school curriculum, and the roles played by English and the foreign language. As already indicated, goals may vary from that of exposing children to the foreign language and culture (FLEX programs) to that of developing near-native proficiency (immersion programs). Similarly, the nature of integration of the language program with the total curriculum varies from supplemental (FLEX and some FLES programs) to integral (immersion and some FLES programs). Finally, the foreign language may be used as the target of instruction (FLEX and FLES programs) or the medium of instruction (some FLES and immersion programs). An understanding of this diversity of program types is essential, both for interpreting research evidence from existing early foreign language programs and for planning appropriately for the establishment of additional programs.

Chapter 2
Rationale for Early Foreign Language Study

Defining the state of the art of foreign language instruction in the elementary school requires an analysis of the rationale for early foreign language study. Given that there have been two "waves" of early foreign language programs in U.S. public schools in the past three decades, it is appropriate to examine the justification for each of the waves of program establishment.

EARLY FOREIGN LANGUAGE PROGRAMS IN THE 1950s AND 1960s

With an awareness in the 1950s of the necessity for international communication came a recognition of the value of foreign language study in general in accomplishing two purposes: first, to produce individuals who were fluent in a foreign language and, second, to provide these individuals with the cultural knowledge essential for cross-cultural communication (Stern, 1963). Further, it was assumed that fluency in a foreign language and knowledge of a foreign culture would both bring about an understanding of and appreciation for the speakers of that foreign language.

Optimal Age

During this period of heightened importance of foreign language instruction, numerous linguists and

psychologists held that children are better second
language learners than adults (Langer, 1958). Not
only were children thought to learn another language
more quickly than adults, but also they were believed
to learn it better. Certainly there was much anec-
dotal evidence to support this concept of an optimal
period for second language acquisition. Children
often seem to "osmose" a second language, apparently
effortlessly and without formal training. Further,
individuals who learn second languages before puberty
quite often exhibit nativelike fluencies that older
language learners do not.

Audio-Lingual Method

Accompanying the belief that children are
superior language learners was the position that the
best language teaching method had been developed. The
audio-lingual method (ALM), which represents the union
of behavioral psychology and descriptive linguistics,
has as a basic tenet the concept that language
learning is a process of habit formation (Prator &
Celce-Murcia, 1979). Thus, ALM activities emphasize
mimicry and memorization, and include a great deal of
manipulation of basic sentence patterns. Vocabulary
is strictly controlled, with more attention given to
form than content.

The existence of the "ideal" method, coupled with
the strong belief in children's superior aptitude for
second language learning, paved the way for a rapid
increase in the number of early foreign language
programs in the late '50s and early '60s. Certainly
the passage of the National Defense Education Act in
1958, with its allocation of funds for foreign language teaching, did much to foster the proliferation
of programs. Unfortunately, the "honeymoon" period
for early foreign language programs was relatively
short-lived. The high expectations of fluency within
relatively short periods of time were not being
fulfilled. Children did not learn as quickly or as
easily as anticipated; ALM did not deliver the pro-
mised results. One problem, according to Page (1966),
was the failure of most programs to adapt teaching

techniques to the level of cognitive development of the students. Another issue was the lack of appropriate evaluation measures for identifying strengths and weaknesses in programs (McLaughlin, 1978). Further, a lack of continuation, or "articulation," of the elementary school program in middle school and high school programs, as well as a lack of trained personnel and instructional materials, contributed to the problems of FLES programs. These unexpected problems, coupled with reduced funding, resulted in a drastic decrease in the number of programs offered throughout the country.

EARLY FOREIGN LANGUAGE PROGRAMS IN THE 1980s

After a hiatus of nearly 15 years, the number of early foreign language programs is on the rise again. The reasons for the current focus on foreign language education are not unlike those cited in the 1950s. The ability to communicate with other language groups is considered essential in both economic and political arenas. The report of the President's Commission on Foreign Language and International Studies (1979) has highlighted the shortcomings of public schools in the United States in this area. Concern about the overwhelming lack of foreign language preparation, coupled with the recent reexamination of public education in general, decidedly accounts for the renewal of interest in foreign language education.

Optimal Age Revisited

While the current interest in foreign language education in general can be readily explained, what accounts for the reemergence of early foreign language programs? Certainly the cornerstones of the earlier growth period--namely, the twin beliefs in the superiority of children as language learners and in the infallibility of ALM--are no longer accepted without question. Concerning the issue of the optimal age for second language acquisition, for example, many researchers and practitioners accept Stern's (1976) position that each age is characterized by particular advantages and disadvantages for language learning. Certainly current second language acquisition research and theory support this concept.

With respect to pronunciation, for instance, Oyama (1976) found that the youngest arrivals to the United States (that is, individuals who began their second language learning at the earliest age) had the least accent; the length of time in country (i.e., the amount of study of the second language and in it) had no effect. Studies by Seliger, Krashen, and Ladefoged (1975) and by Asher and Garcia (1969) reaffirm the importance of age of arrival to native-like pronunciation. Thus "the younger, the better" seems to hold for pronunciation.

Regarding morphology and syntax, however, older learners appear to have the advantage, at least with respect to rate of acquisition. In a study of English-speaking children and adults learning Dutch in the Netherlands, C. Snow and Hoefnagel-Hohle (1977) concluded that older learners had an advantage over younger ones in acquiring morphology and syntax; however, teenagers performed better than adults. Two other studies present findings consistent with these. Fathman (1975) found that older children (ages 11-15) outscored younger learners (ages 6-10) on tests involving morphology and syntax. In a 1974 study, Ervin-Tripp's older subjects (from a group of 4-9-year-olds) scored higher than the younger ones on morphology and syntax tasks.

A similar pattern of advantages and disadvantages emerges in broader comparisons across age groups of language learners. Older learners, for example, have certain cognitive advantages over younger learners. Genesee (1978a) cites the older learner's greater experience and ability in problem solving; Taylor (1974) stresses the adult's superiority in comprehending the abstractness of language.

In the affective domain, however, younger learners may have the advantage. Young children tend to be less inhibited than adults and, therefore, less afraid to make mistakes in a second language--a natural and

necessary part of second language learning. Further,
young children generally do not have negative attitudes toward particular languages or language groups
that could deter learning (Macnamara, 1975). On the
other hand, adolescents may be more self-conscious and
inhibited than young children, whether as the result
of the development of a language ego (Guiora, Brannon,
& Dull, 1972) or of peer group pressure (Brown, 1980).
Such self-consciousness and inhibition may impede language acquisition (Schumann, 1975).

Second Language Acquisition Theory

    While the issue of the optimal age for second
language acquisition may not be quite as clear-cut as
it was believed to be 25 years ago, views of ALM and
its claims about the nature of second language
learning have changed much more drastically. No
longer is second language learning thought to be a
process of "good" habit formation. Chomsky (1965)
argues for the innateness and creativity of language
acquisition. Dulay, Burt, and Krashen (1982) refer to
creative construction, an innate, "subconscious process by which language learners gradually organize the
language they hear, according to rules that they
construct to generate sentences" (p. 11). Further,
Krashen (1981, 1983) makes an important theoretical
distinction between acquisition and learning. Second
language acquisition is a natural and subconscious
process similar to that of first language acquisition.
Conversely, second language learning is the result of
conscious study of the rules, or grammar, of a language. Most importantly, Krashen claims that acquisition is preferable to learning when near-native
competencies are desired.
    Another recent contribution to the corpus of
second language acquisition theory is the concept of
optimal input (Krashen, 1981, 1983). According to
Krashen, the target language available in the environment is far greater than the input, or the amount that
the learner, because of his or her limited proficiency, is able to "take in" for processing. Optimal
input has several characteristics. First, it is

comprehensible. Moreover, for acquisition to occur, the input must contain structures that are slightly above the student's current level of competence. Next, optimal input is interesting and relevant and occurs in sufficient quantities. As is true of the input a first language learner receives, optimal input for a second language learner is not grammatically sequenced. Finally, optimal input provides the learner with "conversational tools," the linguistic means for communicating with native speakers in the target language community.

While Long (1980, 1981) accepts the significance of optimal input in second language acquisition, he contends that negotiated interaction is a prerequisite of second language acquisition. By interacting verbally with native speakers of the target language, learners are able to negotiate input that satisfies the criteria of optimal input specified by Krashen. Without such interaction and the input it provides, the student will not attain proficiency in the second language.

In addition to the critical role that input and interaction play in second language learning, numerous researchers and theoreticians attest to the importance of affective variables (Asher, 1977; Brown, 1980; Curran, 1976; Krashen, 1983; Lozanov, 1979). Learners who, for whatever reasons, feel uncomfortable or unmotivated simply do not achieve as well as those who do not. Thus, a learning environment with what Krashen (1981, 1983) terms a low "affective filter" is desirable.

Also important to second language acquisition, as research evidence indicates, is the provision of a silent period in the curriculum. Children learning both first and second languages in natural settings have been observed to begin producing utterances in the target language only after a period of developing receptive skills. Current second language acquisition theory holds that this silent period is desirable, if not necessary, in a formal setting as well. Methodologies, such as Total Physical Response (TPR), that incorporate a silent period have been shown to be superior on a number of measures of English skills to methodologies that do not (Asher, 1972; Asher, 1977; Asher, Kusudo, & de la Torre, 1974).

Finally, Cummins (1980) has made a theoretical distinction that directly addresses the issue of children learning a second language in a formal setting. Cummins posits the existence of two kinds of language skills in both first and second language: basic interpersonal communicative skills (BICS) and cognitive/academic language proficiency (CALP). Language skills that learners use in "everyday" conversations are BICS. On the other hand, CALP represents language skills that are specifically needed to perform effectively in an academic environment.

If current second language acquisition theory is accepted, it is wise to consider how capable FLEX, FLES, and immersion programs are of providing environments that facilitate second language acquisition. With respect to the issue of acquisition versus learning, there is no doubt that an immersion program, where the second language is used as the medium of instruction, most readily allows for acquisition. However, the teaching in both FLEX and FLES programs can certainly be designed to emphasize acquisition rather than learning. As for optimal input, an immersion program again most easily meets this criterion. Once again, however, both FLEX and FLES programs can provide material that is interesting, relevant, comprehensible, and not grammatically sequenced; their shortcoming is that the requirement of sufficient quantity most likely will not be met. Similarly, while the teaching in FLEX and FLES programs can be structured to foster negotiated interaction, immersion programs--because of the long amounts of time spent using the second language as a medium of instruction-- best create an opportunity for this essential aspect of second language acquisition. Next, both a positive affective environment and a silent period can be provided by all three program types. The former depends on the teacher, the latter on the design of the curriculum. Finally, while BICS can be developed in all three programs, in general only immersion programs allow for the development of CALP. In short, while one program type may more readily provide an environment that facilitates second language acquisition, all three program types can be designed to provide the most facilitative environments possible.

Current Methodologies

Given the relationship of theory and practice, it is not surprising that a number of teaching methodologies and approaches have evolved that incorporate these empirical findings and theoretical positions. As already indicated, TPR (Asher, 1979) includes a silent period, as do the Silent Way (Gattegno, 1972) and the Natural Approach (Krashen & Terrell, 1983; Terrell, 1977). Approaches such as the Natural Approach, Counseling-Learning/Community Language Learning (Curran, 1976), and Suggestopedia (Lozanov, 1979) emphasize low-anxiety environments. Of the methods mentioned, TPR and the Natural Approach have been demonstrated to be the most appropriate for younger language learners (Chamot & McKeon, 1984).

SUMMARY

To the question, "Why foreign language study?" the answer for both the first and second waves of early foreign language programs is virtually the same: to understand and communicate better with speakers of other languages, whether for reasons of defense, politics, or economics. However, to the question, "Why early foreign language study?" the responses for the two phases differ. During the 1950s and 1960s, "early" meant best. Not only was the maxim of "the earlier the better" accepted, but it was believed that ALM was the epitome of effective language teaching approaches. Today, however, early foreign language programs may be established, not because of a belief in the inherent superiority of children as language learners, but because of a desire to provide students with as long an association with another language as possible. Further, few educators today will argue for the infallibility of a particular language teaching methodology. Instead, program planners today have at their disposal more theoretical and empirical data to guide them in selecting methodologies and program types appropriate to their goals. Thus the most appropriate question for educators today is not, "Why establish early foreign language programs?" but rather, "How should early foreign language programs be conducted?" The following chapters contain a range of answers to this question.

Chapter 3
Evidence From Early Foreign Language Programs

A description of the state of the art of foreign language education in the elementary school requires an examination of research evidence from established programs. The results of both experimental studies and program evaluations are pertinent. As in Chapter 2, findings from earlier programs will be discussed separately from more recent findings. The data that are available will be presented according to the program types outlined in Chapter 1.

PROGRAMS IN THE 1950s AND 1960s

As already suggested, early foreign language programs established in the United States in the 1950s and 1960s, if viewed as a whole, did not succeed as anticipated. There were, however, some notable exceptions. Brega and Newell (1965), for example, compared the performance of high school students who had been exposed to French in the elementary grades with that of regular French III (non-FLES) students on the Modern Language Association (MLA) Cooperative tests of listening comprehension, speaking, reading, and writing. The FLES group performed significantly better on all four MLA tests than the group who began French in high school.

In addition, an extensive FLES evaluation was carried out in the public school system of Fairfield, Conn., in 1968 (Oneto, 1968b). The purpose of the study was to investigate the degree to which the teaching of foreign languages in elementary school can produce language skills in high school graduates that are significantly superior to those of graduates whose only language study was in high school. When compared with previous studies, this study was unique because former FLES students in grades 9-12 were, for the most part, assigned to "continuing" classes separate from students who began learning a foreign language in high school. French and Spanish skills in speaking, reading, writing, and listening of students in grades 10, 11, and 12 were measured with the MLA-Cooperative tests.

The study concluded that: (a) pupils who begin continuous study of a foreign language in grade three can achieve, in most instances, significantly greater skill in reading, writing, speaking, and understanding the language than their peers who begin language study in high school; (b) in the audio-lingual skills, high school sophomores who study a foreign language continuously from the third grade may be equal to or better than students two grades ahead of them who begin language study in high school; and (c) high school students who study a foreign language continuously from the third grade may be as skillful in reading and writing the language as students one grade ahead of them who begin language study in high school.

Despite these noteworthy examples, students in early FLES programs overall did not learn as quickly or as well as expected. In fact, the results of many early foreign language programs were so discouraging that 25 percent of those school districts recently surveyed indicated that they had once had programs, but currently do not (Rhodes, 1981). What can account for the poor ratings of these first early foreign language programs?

One problem in attempting to answer this question is the relative lack of data about these programs. Despite the fact that the programs were clearly innovative and, therefore, experimental, most programs were established without an evaluation component (Andersson, 1969). In general, longitudinal studies were not undertaken, nor were comparative studies analyzing different programmatic approaches. The studies that are available from this era often evaluate the instructor's facility with ALM (Pillet, 1974). Thus, whether for lack of an appropriately designed evaluation component or any evaluation component at all, it is difficult to state with any certainty what aspect (or aspects) of the first early foreign language programs accounted for their problems--or, in some instances, their successes.

The most obvious explanation, in retrospect, is that the goals of early programs were unrealistically high. Nativelike fluency on the part of the children was expected, if not demanded, in relatively short periods of time. Given what is now known about the second language acquisition process, these goals were especially inappropriate in the FLES context. FLES programs, in general, offered too few contact hours, providing neither sufficient exposure to the target language for optimal input nor the opportunity for negotiated interaction. Further, in Cummins' terms, only BICS were developed, while the entire domain of language usage (CALP) that is deemed necessary for second language competence in an academic setting was overlooked.

In addition to the problem of unrealistic goals paired with an inappropriate program type, there is the issue of methodology. Since, at first, few theoreticians or practitioners questioned the effectiveness of ALM, pedagogical efforts emphasized perfecting the method rather than developing additional or alternative approaches. Again, in light of current second language acquisition theory, ALM is deficient. In ALM, learning rather than acquisition is the focus; a silent period is not included. Materials stress form, not meaning, and are therefore not always relevant or interesting from the student's perspective. In addition, the materials are grammatically sequenced and generally do not provide the necessary conversational tools. Finally, with its attention to correctness of form and, thus, avoidance of errors, ALM does not foster a low-anxiety language learning environment.

In sum, the first early foreign language programs established in the United States provided relatively little evidence of their strengths or explanations for their weaknesses. Conclusions may be drawn only in retrospect by analyzing program outcomes in light of current second language acquisition theory and empirical research.

CURRENT PROGRAMS

FLEX

Given the renewal of early foreign language programs, what evidence now exists regarding their effectiveness? A response to this question is best formulated by examining each type of program currently established. FLEX programs may be addressed quite quickly. Since they are the most recent of the program types to be developed, virtually no research evidence exists to support or refute their validity. An exception is the report by Lipton (1979), which attests to the effectiveness of a FLEX program. Certain program descriptions are, however, available (Rhodes, 1983).

FLES

Many descriptions of FLES programs are available that detail their goals, objectives, curriculums, and methodologies in a variety of locations, such as Baltimore, Md. (Walker, 1984) and Monterey, Calif. (Garcia & Grady, 1984); and in various languages, such as French (Kodjak & Hayser, 1982), German (Lalande & Taylor, 1982), and Spanish (Bagg, Oates, & Zucker, 1984). Certain empirical data are available as well.

In addition to the Brega and Newell (1965) and Oneto (1968b) studies already cited, a study by Karabinus (1976) compared performance on four special auditory tests in groups of fifth-, sixth-, and seventh-graders who had FLES beginning in the fifth grade with that of fifth-, sixth-, and seventh-graders who had had no foreign language instruction. At all grade levels, the means on "Auditory Memory of Content" were significantly higher for FLES students than for students not in foreign language programs. Thus, although the body of research data on FLES programs is not large, empirical evidence suggests that students who participate in FLES programs perform better in the long run on a number of measures than those who do not.

Immersion

Although the evidence for FLES programs is tentatively positive, that for immersion programs--at least for language majority students--is overwhelmingly positive. While evaluations of immersion programs in the United States are still relatively few, Canadian researchers have been diligently documenting the linguistic, cognitive, and social effects on participating students since the inception of the programs in Canada. Thus, the corpus of available data is large, and can be examined with respect to the stated program goals--first and second language development, academic achievement, and psychological and social development.

Results related to native language development will be discussed first. In no instance has a difference been shown between the oral English skills of immersion and nonimmersion students (Swain, 1984a). This is undoubtedly due to the pervasive presence of English in the school, community, and home environments. Regarding literacy-related skills, however, the picture is somewhat different. Early total immersion students are initially behind their nonimmersion counterparts. Yet, within a year of the introduction of English-language arts, immersion students perform as well on standardized English achievement tests as the comparison students (Genesee, 1978b). Second- and third-grade early partial immersion students perform less well on certain English literacy-related skills than their English-program peers (Barik, Swain, & Nwanunobi, 1977). One possible explanation is that the simultaneous teaching of literacy skills as is done in early partial programs causes confusion for a period of time (Swain, 1984a). If so, it is preferable to teach initial literacy skills in only one language.

Other studies of first language development reveal valuable information as well. Genesee (1974), in a study of the writing of fourth-grade immersion students, found that the immersion group scored lower than the comparison group on spelling but higher on measures of creativity. Lapkin (1982), in a study of the global assessment of fifth-graders' compositions, found no difference between experimental and control groups. In a parent survey conducted by McEachern (1980), 80 percent of the parents with children in immersion programs felt that their children were experiencing no problems in English communication. Finally, children in kindergarten, first-grade, and second-grade immersion programs have been judged superior to nonimmersion students on measures of communicative effectiveness (Genesee, Tucker, & Lambert, 1975).

Studies on academic achievement and cognitive development will be examined next. Swain and Lapkin (1982) reviewed standardized mathematics tests of early total immersion students, grades one through eight. On average, the students scored equal to or better than their nonimmersion counterparts on 35 of 38 tests. Similarly, on 14 administrations of a standardized science test, early total immersion students, grades five through eight, and nonimmersion students scored equally well.

Similar to the findings related to first language development, performance by students in programs other than early total immersion is often less than consistent. Barik and Swain (1977) report inferior mathematics scores for early partial immersion students beginning in the third grade. In addition, Barik and Swain (1978) found inferior performance by early partial immersion students in science beginning at the fifth-grade level.

As for students in late immersion programs, Barik and Swain (1976) observed occasional inferior performance in science when the experimental groups had received only one or two years' instruction in French as a second language before beginning the immersion program. A similar phenomenon was observed in mathematics performance (Barik, Swain, & Gaudino, 1976). On the other hand, late immersion students, who had received French instruction yearly before entering a program, performed as well in content areas as the comparison groups (Genesee, Polich, & Stanley, 1977).

Several studies suggest cognitive benefits of bilingualism that develops in immersion programs, though these benefits are not associated with specific content areas. In a seven-year study of immersion and nonimmersion students matched for IQ and socioeconomic status, Scott (1973, reported in Lambert, 1984) found that the fifth- and sixth-grade immersion students scored higher on divergent thinking, a measure of cognitive flexibility. Further, Barik and Swain (1976) and Cummins (1975, reported in Lambert, 1984; 1976) found increases in students' IQs or in divergent thinking that were not present in the comparison groups. Finally, students whose IQs are below average or who have learning disabilities are not at any more of a disadvantage in immersion programs than they are in all-English programs (Bruck, 1979; Genesee, 1976; Swain, 1975). In fact, Bruck (1978) suggests that, at least with respect to French language acquisition, learning-disabled students in immersion programs may have an advantage. While these studies are indeed significant, there is no doubt that much research remains to be done on the relationship between bilingualism and cognitive processes.

Numerous benefits from immersion programs have been documented in the areas of psychological and social development. Lambert and Tucker (1972), for example, found that immersion students have more positive attitudes toward French Canadians than their nonimmersion English-Canadian peers. Cziko, Lambert, and Gutter (1979) report that immersion programs appear to reduce English Canadians' perception of the social distance between themselves and French Canadians. Fifth- and sixth-grade immersion students, when asked to write a composition on why they liked (or did not like) being Canadian, more frequently mentioned the linguistic and cultural diversity of Canada. Nonimmersion students tended to cite the natural beauty of the country (Swain, 1980). Clearly, then, the goal of increased cultural understanding apears to be a by-product of immersion programs.

Ironically, one of the most important goals of immersion programs, that of achieving competence in the second language, appears to be the most problematic. For example, when the French performance of early total immersion students is compared with that of nonimmersion students who receive French as a second language, immersion students are consistently superior (Swain, 1984a). However, when compared with native speakers of French, the immersion groups appear to need six or seven years to achieve average performance in the receptive skills of listening and reading (Swain & Lapkin, 1982). Furthermore, immersion students have not shown native-like proficiency in productive skills (speaking and writing) (Genesee, 1978b; Harley, 1979, 1982; Spilka, 1976). Finally, Plann (1976), in a U.S. study, surmised that students develop classroom dialects peculiar to their immersion programs by reinforcing each other's incorrect usage.

All of the studies cited, with the exception of the last, are Canadian. Few studies on immersion programs in the United States exist, first because of a paucity of programs, and second because of a lack of financial support for such research. However, the Culver City Spanish Immersion Program, because of its association with the University of California-Los Angeles, has been evaluated. (See, for example, Boyd, 1974; Campbell, 1972; Cathcart, 1972; Cohen, 1974a, 1974b, 1975a; Cohen, Fier, & Flores, 1973; Galvan, 1978; Lebach, 1974.) Findings basically replicate those of Canadian programs (Campbell, 1984). Academically, immersion students have performed equally as well as or better than their nonimmersion peers. Their English skills are equivalent, with the exception of mechanics and spelling. Some attitudinal improvement is evident. Their Spanish, however, while competent, is not nativelike.

Program Comparison

In addition to the studies of particular program types, one recent study has compared the performance of students participating in different types of programs. Gray, Rhodes, Campbell, and Snow (1984) compared the foreign language achievement of students in FLES, partial immersion, and total immersion programs. In addition, the achievement of these groups was compared with that of high school foreign language students.

Students learning French in immersion programs significantly outperformed those in FLES in all four skill areas on the MLA test. Further, compared with high school students, immersion students scored at the 80th percentile in listening (i.e., 80% of the high school students scored lower), while FLES students scored at the 14th percentile. Also, immersion students ranked high compared with high school students in speaking (99th percentile) and reading (77th percentile).

Trends were similar for the Spanish group. Immersion students outperformed partial immersion students on all four subtests; partial immersion subjects, in turn, outperformed their FLES peers. Differences are significant in listening and speaking when FLES and partial immersion students are compared. When immersion and partial immersion students are compared, differences are significant in all skill areas except speaking. In comparison with high school students, Spanish immersion students scored above the 70th percentile in all four skill areas. Both partial immersion and FLES students scored comparatively well in speaking.

Thus, at least with respect to the overall foreign language proficiency of the students, it is obvious which program type is the most effective: "Immersion, setting the most ambitious language fluency goals, provides the highest level of proficiency. Partial immersion ranks second in promoting proficiency attainment, and FLES, whose goals are the least ambitious, ranks third" (Rhodes & Snow, 1984, pp. 4-5).

INTERPRETATION OF FINDINGS

Given the sheer volume of evidence available that supports immersion programs, as well as the outcome of

the comparative study just discussed, the apparent
logical conclusion is that immersion programs are the
most appropriate if native-like fluency is the goal.
An immersion program is the vehicle that can deliver
the best results. However, a few words of caution are
in order.

Each program type--immersion, FLES, and FLEX--has
its particular goals with respect to both the level of
fluency and the number of skills to be developed.
Just as each set of goals may have validity within a
particular educational context, so does each program
type have validity with respect to a school district's
stated foreign language goals. The issue, then, is
not necessarily to determine which early foreign language program is inherently the best, but rather which
is the most appropriate to a district's goals. An
additional issue is to determine the critical features
that will ensure success for a program.

UNANSWERED QUESTIONS

These questions represent the "tip of the
iceberg" when it comes to the nature of optimal early
foreign language programs. Many more questions need
investigating, including the following: All things
considered, what is the best age to begin a foreign
language program? In FLEX, how many languages can be
effectively introduced in a year? How much target
language exposure per day and week is best in a FLES
approach? What methodologies are most appropriate for
children? Which methods, if any, are more effective
with younger children; with older children? Do all
program types foster positive attitudes toward the
target languages and their speakers? Are instructors
with little foreign language background really effective as FLEX teachers? What influence do the attitudes of parents, teachers, and administrators have on
the success of programs? Does early foreign language
study enhance native language performance? Are immersion programs as effective in the United States as in
Canada? If not, what are the variables involved?

As these questions are only a representative
sampling of the body of questions that must be
addressed, it is perhaps safe to predict that answers
will be slow in coming. Even if funding were readily
available, research would still be hampered to a
degree by the lack of language assessment instruments
that are appropriate for children and by lack of consistency across program types.

SUMMARY

More data are available on the efficacy of recent
early foreign language programs than from those first
established. Despite the greater volume of information and the validity of the findings, however,
further research is clearly needed. Nonetheless, as a
result of the work of second language theoreticians
and researchers, educators are certainly in a better
position now to make informed decisions on programs
and curricula than they were 25 years ago.

Chapter 4
Program Implementation

Before establishing an early foreign language program in a school district, careful advance planning is required. While there is no single approach to program implementation, one will be highlighted in this chapter as an example. Essential steps in this program approach are (a) establishing a steering committee, (b) determining the extent of support for a program, (c) defining goals and program design, and (d) estimating the human and material resources that will be needed and the administrative costs that will be involved. In addition, a district must consider who will participate, the nature of the curriculum, and evaluation procedures.

ESTABLISHMENT OF A STEERING COMMITTEE

A steering committee selected to investigate the feasibility of a foreign language program at the elementary school level might comprise a representative or representatives from each of the following groups: parents, teachers, and administrators. Parental participation is crucial. Evidence from Canadian immersion programs shows that one of the factors in the success of such programs is the involvement of parents from the earliest stages of program development (Tucker, 1980). Faculty and administrative support is, of course, essential as well, not only to the establishment of a program, but also to its continued acceptance and growth. In essence, the steering committee has three responsibilities:

1. to become well informed about the nature of early foreign language programs, including the advantages and the limitations of each type;

2. to serve as an information-gathering body regarding the particular needs and resources of the school district; and

3. to develop a detailed plan of the proposed program to submit to parents, teachers, and administrators for approval.

Several means exist for steering committee members to become informed about early foreign language programs. The most obvious is to do as much background reading as possible on the subject. In addition to the language- or district-specific articles mentioned in Chapter 3, a number of general sources are available (see the listing of curriculum guides that starts on p. 105). Fairfax County Public Schools (1978; 1982), for example, have produced two guides, one a handbook for program development, and the other a compilation of resources. Also available is *Foreign Language in the Elementary School: A Practical Guide* (Rhodes & Schreibstein, 1983), which contains an overview of program types and specific suggestions for implementation procedures. Another source is the report entitled "Elementary School Foreign Language Instruction in the United States: Innovative Approaches for the 1980s" (Rhodes, Tucker, & Clark, 1981), which includes descriptions of a variety of program types currently in operation throughout the country. Finally, if a district is interested primarily in immersion programs, a comprehensive source is *Studies on Immersion Education. A Collection for United States Educators* (California State Department of Education, 1984).

Other ways for steering committee members to become more knowledgeable about early foreign language instruction involve inservice training and on-site

visits. Given the commitment involved in mounting a
new program, it is often desirable (and cost
effective) for a district to hire a consultant who is
a foreign language expert to instruct the members of
the steering committee. The same consultant could be
employed at a later time to aid in presenting the proposed program to groups of parents, teachers, and
administrators. In addition to receiving inservice
training, steering committee members may observe
programs already in operation in nearby districts.
Personnel in school districts operating innovative
programs are usually accustomed to visitors and
willing to share information.

Equipped with information gathered through
reading, inservice training, and on-site visits,
steering committee members are then ready to make
informed decisions, as well as to serve as resources
for district personnel and community members who may
have questions or concerns about the proposed program.
With respect to the other two responsibilities identified for a steering committee (namely, to serve as a
data-gathering body and to write a program proposal),
the following sections will serve to illustrate the
nature of these duties.

DETERMINATION OF SUPPORT

Once steering committee members have acquired the
necessary background information, their next key step
is to determine the extent of support for an early
foreign language program. A questionnaire for parents
is recommended. Such a survey should ascertain
whether parents believe in the importance of foreign
language education in general, and in foreign language
education in the elementary school in particular. A
survey of parents in the San Diego area, for example,
found that 82% believed the city school system should
offer foreign language instruction at the elementary
level; further, 46% of those polled were willing to
pay for the instruction (Rickards, 1984). The
questionnaire should also determine the parents' pre-

ferred goals for foreign language instruction, such as exposure to or fluency in another language. Questionnaire writers may wish to include brief descriptions of program types at this point to illustrate how specific goals are matched to program types. Detailed explanations are, however, not desirable in this type of format or at this point in the program development process (Rhodes & Schreibstein, 1983). Finally, the survey should serve to identify the language or languages that parents think should be taught.

In addition to surveying parents of potential program participants, it is also essential to determine the degree of support that exists among the teachers whose students will be affected. A formal questionnaire may again be used as the information-gathering tool. It is important to learn whether teachers have positive attitudes toward foreign language instruction. If so, which language(s) do they favor for instruction? Do the teachers believe the foreign language program should be available to all students? If not, who should be eligible for participation? If a program is offered, should it be scheduled before or after the school day, or should it become an established part of the school day? If the latter is the case, what existing areas of study should be reduced or replaced? How do teachers envision their participation in the program? For example, will a teacher actively participate in the foreign language activities along with the students, and attempt to integrate relevant information with other subjects being taught; or does that teacher intend to use the students' time with the foreign language specialist as an opportunity for grading papers or planning lessons? While teachers are generally supportive of foreign language instruction, that support can easily turn to opposition if such a program adversely affects their teaching duties. For this reason, a steering committee must assess the attitudes of the teachers who will be affected.

No less important is a determination of the extent of support for an early foreign language program on the part of school administrators. Baranick (1985), for example, has shown the important role that principals play as "gatekeepers" in foreign language

programs. With administrators, a questionnaire may be
less effective than other means of data gathering.
Informal interviews may be used to assess the degree
of support or opposition. Another way is to have the
steering committee make a formal presentation to
school board members and administrators in order to
explain the functions of the committee and to request
a detailed statement of support, with answers to
questions such as the following: Do administrators
believe in the necessity of foreign language education? Do they believe the elementary school to be the
appropriate level at which to begin instruction? What
language(s) do they think are important for students
in the district to learn? In addition, will school
officials support an innovative program only if no
additional costs are involved or if outside funding is
obtained, or are they willing to commit funds to such
a project? For how long will officials support a
pilot program: one year, three years, five years?
While such specifics may be finalized only after a
detailed proposal is presented, it is nonetheless
important to the decision-making process of the
steering committee to ascertain the limitations of
administrative support ahead of time.

DEFINITION OF GOALS AND OBJECTIVES

Once the results of the surveys of parents,
teachers, and administrators have been compiled, the
steering committee should concern itself with the task
of defining goals for the proposed program. Three
basic questions should be asked. First, which skill
areas do the polled groups believe should be
developed: listening and speaking only, or listening,
speaking, reading, and writing? Next, what level of
proficiency within each of the designated skill areas
should be attained by participating students? Moreover, should proficiency be expected in conversational
as well as academic language usage? Finally, what
level of cultural awareness should be fostered by the
program? The desired pedagogical result in each of

these areas should be clearly stated as a program
goal.

After goals have been identified for the proposed
early foreign language program, specific program
objectives may be formulated. Since program objectives are closely tied to the curriculum, this particular responsibility may be shared with or delegated
to a curriculum committee. (See the later section on
"Development of Curriculum.") The compatibility of
program objectives with goals should be carefully examined. Take, for example, a FLES program that has as
a stated goal to develop "rudimentary conversational
skills" in a given language. Among the objectives
that would facilitate achieving this goal might be the
following:

> By the end of the academic year, students will be
> able to:
>
> 1. give basic greetings;
>
> 2. count from 1 to 100;
>
> 3. give their names, addresses, telephone num-
>   bers, and ages; and
>
> 4. ask and understand questions involving <u>who</u>,
>   <u>what</u>, <u>where</u>, and <u>when</u>.

As already mentioned, one possible reason for the
demise of many of the first early foreign language
programs was the establishment of unrealistically
ambitious goals. Another possibility is that when
goals and objectives were not clearly delineated,
misunderstandings arose as to the expected levels of
fluency and cultural awareness. Clearly, it behooves
program planners to be as explicit as possible in the
statement of goals and objectives so that all who will
be involved with the program have a sound understanding of its nature and realistic expectations of its
outcomes.

Whatever goals are set by the steering committee in response to survey results will directly indicate which program type is to be selected. For example, if the consensus is that exposure to one or more foreign language and cultures is desirable, then a FLEX program is appropriate. If, on the other hand, school personnel and parents prefer the development of oral (and, perhaps, written) proficiency in addition to cultural awareness, then a FLES program is in order. Finally, an immersion program is called for if the highest levels of proficiency are to be attained, and if parents and school officials alike support the teaching of content subjects in a language other than English.

Even though there is a direct correlation between stated goals and program type, programmatic decisions must be made regarding each approach. If a FLEX format is chosen, for example, will the sessions be a part of the school day or additional? What number of sessions per week and minutes per session is optimal? Which students, classes, grades, or schools will participate? These same questions apply to the design of FLES programs.

With respect to curriculum-integrated FLES programs, it is obvious that the classes will be a part of the scheduled school day. Yet, decisions must be made regarding the number of contact days per week (three? five?) and the amount of instructional time per contact (30 minutes? 45 minutes?). More importantly, which parts of the existing curriculum may complement the foreign language program? Again, which students, classes, grades, or schools will participate in the program?

Immersion programs, of course, require the most complex program design. Does the district prefer a total or partial immersion plan? If the former, all content area subjects will be taught in the target language at the outset of the program. If the latter, planners must decide which subjects are to be taught in English and which in the target language. Does the district prefer an early, delayed, or late program?

Again, which classes and students will be involved?

In addition to the questions of integration of a selected program with the total school day, there is the critical issue of articulation of the program across grade levels. If a student studies German in a FLES program, for instance, are advanced levels of German available when that student reaches secondary school? Is foreign language instruction offered at the junior high level? Is there an appropriate course of study available for students exiting from immersion programs? With respect to this last question, guidelines from the Center for Applied Linguistics in Washington, D.C., recommend that students participating in immersion programs in elementary school should receive "at least one course each year in junior and senior high taught in the foreign language" (Rhodes, Tucker, & Clark, 1981, p. 40). The entire sequence of foreign language offerings in grades K-12 should be reviewed when an administration plans to introduce an early foreign language program.

IDENTIFICATION OF RESOURCES

Given the goals that a steering committee establishes, what resources--both human and material--are needed to accomplish them? As in the previous section, an examination of needed resources by program type is in order.

Teachers

Three factors are involved when considering teachers for an early foreign language program: their fluency in the target language, their language teaching experience, and certification. The relative importance of each of these factors is a function of the type of foreign language program proposed. With respect to FLEX programs, for example, a minimal amount of target language fluency (and, therefore, of language teaching experience) is required on the part

of the teacher. In fact, districts such as
Evansville, Ind., report success with a program that
provides two days of training, self-explanatory
materials, and tapes to classroom teachers with minimal experience with the target language (Rhodes,
Tucker, & Clark, 1981). Since classroom teachers may
be used in this approach, foreign language certification need not be an issue. Other approaches may
be used in FLEX programs, however. A before-school
program in Oak Park, Ill., for example, used a parent
whose Spanish was fluent and who had previously taught
at the elementary level (Bethke, personal communication, February, 1985). Advanced foreign language students at the high school and college levels may be
used as instructors, as well, if credentialing issues
are dealt with (Bagg, Oates, & Zucker, 1984).

Because the goals of FLES programs are more
stringent with respect to language fluency levels than
those of FLEX programs, school districts have less
flexibility regarding the qualifications of the
teacher. A higher level of target language proficiency is needed, and prior language teaching
experience is desirable. Further, elementary certification is usually a necessity if the FLES program
is a part of the scheduled school day. While an occasional community volunteer with the appropriate skills
may be found for a before- or after-school program, it
is virtually always necessary for a district to employ
a foreign language specialist either full or part
time. Many districts are able to find a person with
the appropriate qualifications who is already teaching
within the system (a third-grade teacher who minored
in French, for example); however, reassigning this
teacher would still entail finding a replacement to
perform the teacher's former duties. As for
curriculum-integrated FLES programs, the teacher must
possess an even greater degree of fluency since the
language class is taught in the target language.
Further, since all four skill areas of listening,
speaking, reading, and writing are to be developed,
the teacher must be equally proficient in oral and
written communication.

If the qualifications for a teacher in a
curriculum-integrated program are demanding, they are

even more so for the teacher in an immersion program. Not only must the immersion teacher be highly proficient in both oral and written skills, but that teacher must also be able to teach content area subjects in the target language. Even native speakers of the target language with the proper certification may not have had the training necessary to teach math, science, and social studies. Conversely, a native speaker may be available who has the appropriate language and teaching skills, but not the required teaching credentials. Thus, because of the level of proficiency needed by a teacher in this kind of program, it is not unusual to find a district in the dilemma of having to choose between a native speaker of the target language who has no teaching credentials in this country and a credentialed nonnative speaker of the target language whose abilities in one or more skill areas are insufficient.

Materials

In addition to potential staffing problems, the need for material resources must be carefully considered. Once again, the nature of the support materials needed varies with the program type, as well as with the goals and objectives of the program.

FLEX programs are the least demanding in the materials they require. Since the emphasis is on oral language, photographs, drawings, and objects already in use in the district may be used for language lessons. Single copies of records, tapes, books (to be read aloud by the teacher), and games may be acquired. Although most materials on the market are aimed at high school and college students, a sufficient amount is available for children through foreign language publishers who deal in the more commonly taught languages of Spanish, French, and German.

FLES programs require more materials than FLEX programs, partly because more class time is involved, but also because reading and writing are quite often incorporated. Again, some commercial materials are available in the commonly taught languages; however, relatively few basal series exist that are appropriate

for elementary school students. Thus, the FLES
teacher usually devotes a great deal of time to
adapting materials intended for older students or to
writing original materials. Some districts recognize
the need for systematic materials development because
of this shortage. The Spanish as a Second Language
Gifted Program in Rockford, Ill. (1983), for example,
included materials development as part of the proposed
program model.

Given problems with materials often faced by FLES
programs, it should not be surprising that immersion
programs are often greatly hampered by a lack of
materials. Districts must locate not only language
materials that are appropriate for their students, but
also content area texts in the target language.
Obviously, science, math, and social studies texts are
available from foreign countries. However, very often
these texts, since they are designed for native
speakers, are too difficult for students in immersion
programs, and the content is often not appropriate.

ESTIMATION OF ADMINISTRATIVE COSTS

Certainly, projecting administrative costs is a
key step in the decision-making process of a steering
committee. Given the great variability in cost of
goods and services across the country, it is not useful to discuss dollars and cents. However, certain
variables affecting operating costs will be cited.

A steering committee must, of course, estimate
both the start-up and the continuing costs of instructional personnel, materials, space, and miscellaneous
items. At first glance, it would appear that FLEX
programs are the least expensive and immersion
programs the most expensive in all the areas mentioned. Whether this is true, however, depends on the
individual district involved. For example, a school
district may use volunteers to teach FLEX classes,
thus entailing no expenditure for personnel. However,
if the class is offered before or after the school
day, there may be expenses for heating, air con-
ditioning, and lighting; supervisory and custodial

services; and busing. On the other hand, a district
offering a FLES program may have to purchase relatively few instructional materials, but have to hire a
foreign language specialist. Yet another district
with an immersion program may have to purchase a large
number of materials, but be able to use a teacher with
the desired qualifications who is already employed in
the district.

Additional expenses that a steering committee
will need to consider involve materials development
and evaluation. Will the language teachers be
expected to adapt or write materials as the need
arises, or is it more cost effective in the long run
to provide additional monies (during the summer
months, for example) for curriculum writing? Does the
district employ a full-time evaluator? If not, an
evaluator will need to be contracted to determine
whether a program is functioning according to its
goals. The nature and extent of the desired evaluation will, of course, determine the amount to be
allocated for this expense.

Finally, whether for start-up costs or continuing
expenses, a steering committee may wish to consider
sources of revenue instead of or in addition to the
school district itself. Especially for before- or
after-school programs, for example, a district may
wish to charge a nominal fee for participating students. A parent-teacher organization might organize a
fundraiser to purchase audiovisual equipment or
instructional materials for a district's program.
Occasionally state and federal monies are awarded for
such innovative programs; private foundations may have
grant money available. A local business or industry
with international dealings may agree to cosponsor a
foreign language program. While outside sources of
financial support for educational programs are certainly not abundant, a steering committee should,
nonetheless, investigate potential sources of revenue
as it considers administrative costs of a proposed
early foreign language program.

SELECTION OF PROGRAM PARTICIPANTS

The issue of the selection of program participants will, to a large degree, be determined by the
design of the program discussed earlier. Will all
students in the district, for example, participate, or
only those in one or two schools? If the latter is
the case, what criteria will be used for selecting the
schools--for example, parental support, enthusiasm of
the teaching staff, or the presence of needed
materials and instructional personnel? Also, will a
program be begun simultaneously at several grade
levels, or at a single grade and expanded upward in
subsequent years? What will determine the grade level
or levels of implementation--research evidence or the
other factors just mentioned?

When all students in a class, grade, or school
are targeted for participation in a program, the main
task is basically one of notification of parents and
guardians in order to explain the program. If, however, only certain students will be allowed to participate, the steering committee must devote more time
to determining the criteria for selection. For
example, should the program be voluntary, that is,
open only to those who express an interest? If the
program charges tuition, will subsidies be available
for those interested students who cannot afford to
pay? Should the program be available only to those
students in a particular "track" or who have been
designated as gifted? If so, the program will pro-
bably become known as "elitist"; is this the
district's intention? Should a foreign language aptitude test be devised to identify students who would
particularly benefit from studying a foreign language?
Most importantly, if only particular students will be
allowed to participate, how will the steering committee handle publicity in the community? As with the
other areas of program planning already discussed, the
issue of student selection deserves a great deal of
forethought on the part of the planners.

DEVELOPMENT OF CURRICULUM

While it should not be the responsibility of the
steering committee to develop the curriculum itself,
it is certainly within the purview of the committee to
ensure that this task is assigned to appropriate
people. Whether a separate committee is formed for
curricular decisions, or whether a team of curriculum
writers is selected, several tasks are involved.

First, based on the goals of the program, as well
as on current second language acquisition theory, a
methodology or approach must be agreed on. Then,
materials must be identified that are compatible with
the selected goals and methodologies and appropriate
for the age and grade levels of the students involved.
The search should begin with commercial publishers of
foreign language materials. A second step is to
examine materials that have been produced by school
districts with early foreign language programs already
in operation, such as Milwaukee Public Schools (1982);
Indiana Department of Public Instruction (1981); and
Cincinnati Public Schools (1978a, 1978b, 1978c).
Finally, once certain materials are acquired, they may
need to be modified or supplemented by original
materials to suit the particular student population
involved.

Curriculum development, of course, involves more
than just agreeing on an instructional approach and
selecting or writing materials. Broader issues must
be considered, as well. For example, do the materials
used in the foreign language program complement those
used in the all-English curriculum? Are there obvious
instances in which connections may be made and comple-
mentary units developed? For example, if a fourth-
grade social studies class is studying concepts of
rural and urban living, the French language class may
contrast life in Paris and a village in Burgundy at
the same time.

Another issue that deserves attention is the
articulation of the program from one grade level to
the next. Such continuity may be a particular problem
for districts that begin a foreign language program at
a number of grade levels simultaneously. Are

materials that are suitable for a second-grader in his
or her second year of German study, for instance,
equally suitable for a sixth-grader in the second year
of study? If not, may they be adapted? Further, how
much allowance should be made in materials for
regression over the summer months, during which
children are not exposed to the foreign language?
Finally, are the approaches and materials used in an
elementary foreign language program compatible with
those in a junior high or secondary program? Are
there overlaps or gaps?

In addition to those areas already mentioned, a
curriculum team may choose to investigate resources in
the community that may supplement the curriculum. Are
there native speakers of the target language who can
visit the classroom to give special presentations or
to serve as interlocutors? Are there ethnic
restaurants or movie theaters that show foreign language films? If so, these are ideal sites for field
trips. Is a language immersion weekend (Haynes,
1983), a language camp (Vines, 1983), or a summer
program (Urbanski, 1982) a possibility for the
district? Several school districts in the country have
intensified their students' foreign language experiences with these kinds of supplementary experiences.

Obviously, not all of the curricular con-
siderations so far identified may be determined before
the program gets under way. Certainly, however,
methods and basic materials must be agreed on before-
hand. Key issues with respect to the integration and
articulation of materials may also be identified ahead
of time, with refinements made on an ongoing basis
once the program is in operation.

FORMULATION OF EVALUATION PROCEDURES

Similar to the task of curriculum development,
the responsibility of the formulation of procedures
for program evaluation need not rest solely in the
hands of the steering committee. However, the committee should ensure that the effectiveness of the new

program will be appropriately assessed. Because of
the importance of the evaluation component, as well as
its potential complexities, the topic of evaluation
will be addressed separately in the next chapter.

SUMMARY

Many factors are involved in the process of
implementing an early foreign language program.
First, a steering committee of parents, teachers, and
administrators may be formed to study information
available on early foreign language programs, as well
as to gather data on school and community support,
availability of resources, and estimated costs of
program administration. Program goals and objectives
must be defined, and program design must be formulated. In addition, provisions must be made for the
selection of program participants, the development of
curriculum, and the establishment of evaluation procedures. While the tasks identified may seem overwhelmingly time consuming, it is important to remember
that--as with any new educational program--detailed
and conscientious planning ahead of time generally
results in a smoothly run, effective early foreign
language program.

Chapter 5
Program Evaluation

As mentioned in Chapter 4, one important facet of program implementation is the provision for an evaluation component. Since the first wave of early language programs was characterized both by a lack of evaluations and by inappropriate evaluations, it is essential that current programs receive more careful monitoring. Information from program evaluations is needed to determine the degree of success of early foreign language programs, as well as to identify factors contributing to or impeding that success. The following sections are intended to present basic concepts in evaluation and to suggest necessary steps in the evaluation process. Additional sources of information will be provided in the Summary section.

BASIC CONCEPTS

While the concept of program evaluation is often synonymous with complex designs and elaborate statistical procedures, such need not be the case. In fact, most program evaluations are designed to answer the basic question, "Have the stated program objectives been met?" (Bissell, 1980). As such, the designs are generally straightforward and may involve little or no statistical manipulation. Regardless of the simplicity or complexity of an evaluation design, however, certain key concepts must be considered when planning a program evaluation.

Very basically, program evaluations may vary in

duration, focus, process, and instrumentation. For example, evaluations may be short-term or long-term in duration. In the context of early foreign language programs--as with any educational program, a short-term evaluation is generally synonymous with a single academic year. A typical question on a short-term evaluation study, for example, might be whether 75% of the third-graders scored significantly higher on a given German oral assessment measure at the end of the academic year than at the beginning. Since the cumulative effects of early foreign language training are usually not seen in a single academic year, and since it is, therefore, unwise to make decisions about continuing a program on the basis of the results of a single year, many school districts allow for long-term studies. These long-term evaluations, which generally use data gathered over three to five academic years, may focus on the cumulative effects of early foreign language instruction, such as trends in achievement in certain skills areas.

In addition to differences in duration, program evaluations may differ in focus. Virtually all evaluation designs are concerned with the product of the program (Popham, 1975). That is, they evaluate whether a certain percentage of students achieve the desired gains on particular measures of language proficiency. In short, they ask whether the program in question has produced the intended performance results. In addition, some evaluation designs focus on process (Popham, 1975). For example, if a given early foreign language program has as one of its objectives the inservice training of teachers, the measures evaluate the inservice training that took place. They ask, for example: How many sessions were offered? What were the topics? Did the training improve teachers' performances?

With respect to process, evaluations are generally regarded as formative or summative (California State Department of Education, 1975). Formative evaluations are ongoing; on the basis of data collected throughout the academic year, adjustments in programs may be made without waiting for end-of-the-year information. For instance, a mid-year assessment of the writing skills of fourth-grade students in a French

FLES program may suggest that year-end goals are not likely to be met. As a result, teachers in the program may devote more instructional time to issues of writing. Summative evaluations, on the other hand, are conducted at the end of a program year or at the end of a student's participation in the program. Data gathered from summative evaluations may influence the conduct of the program in subsequent years, but obviously have no effect on the program during the year it is investigated.

Finally, program evaluations vary as to the instrumentation used to collect data. Language assessment instruments range from commercially available, standardized tests to tests that are locally developed and normed. They may be written tests that assess discrete points of the foreign language, or they may be oral interviews that assess a more global knowledge of the foreign language. (Whatever the language assessment instrument used, however, it is important to remember that, because of the complex nature of second language acquisition, no single instrument can be expected to determine infallibly a student's precise level of proficiency.) In addition to language assessment instruments, questionnaires and interviews may be used to measure attitudinal changes or degrees of support for the program on the part of students, teachers, administrators, and parents. Further, observational checklists provide information on teacher competencies, instructional methodologies and activities, and student participation. In all instances mentioned, the usual procedure is to collect data first at the outset of a program or academic year and again at the end. These pre- and posttest data allow comparisons to be made to determine the direction and degree of change with respect to each program objective.

PROCEDURES

Just as program implementation consists of specific steps, so, too, does program evaluation. In essence, program evaluation may be thought of as comprising three phases--the preliminary, the data-gathering, and the analysis and application phase. Each phase, in turn, encompasses a number of activities.

Preliminary Activities

The preliminary phase of a program evaluation entails several activities: selecting an evaluator, establishing the purposes of the evaluation, selecting questions and methods, and scheduling timelines (Bissell, 1980). School districts may differ in the degree of choice they enjoy in selecting an evaluator. In some instances, for example, districts may use a person who functions as part of the program. In other situations, the designated person may be the district evaluator. Finally, districts may choose to hire an outside consultant as the program evaluator. Each choice carries certain advantages and disadvantages. While outside evaluators, for example, require a con-sulting fee that district-related personnel do not, they are generally regarded as more objective than their district-based colleagues. On the other hand, the very distance from the program that supposedly ensures the outside evaluator's objectivity may also result in a misunderstanding of the district and its goals for the students in the foreign language program.

Once an evaluator is chosen, the purposes of the evaluation must be established. Why is the evaluation being conducted--to document students' progress, to judge whether monies are being appropriately spent, to assess teachers' effectiveness, to ascertain the impact of the program on community attitudes, or to determine whether a program should be funded in sub-sequent years? Also, for whom is the evaluation intended--program directors, district administrators, school board officials, or parents?

Obviously, the purposes of the evaluation, in addition to the stated goals of the program, directly affect the choice of evaluation questions. The nature of the evaluation questions, in turn, directly determines the selection of data-gathering methods. For example, the expressed goals of a given FLEX program might include the development of a positive attitude toward language learning in general and toward Spanish in particular. An evaluation of such a program could focus on these two areas for the purposes of showing administrators and parents that the program is achieving its goals and should, therefore, be continued. Given the nature of the topics to be investigated, attitude surveys or interview instruments would most likely be used to gather the necessary data. In another example, a stated objective of a FLES program might be to provide teachers with ongoing training in second language teaching methodology. In order to provide program directors with the information necessary to determine the nature of future training, a portion of the evaluation could focus on the effectiveness of the training. The evaluator could use program records on the amount of training provided, the topics, and the teachers' attendance. In addition, questionnaires could provide information on the teachers' perceptions of the value of the training; classroom observations might determine whether techniques and activities presented in training were being incorporated into the classroom.

After evaluation questions are determined and data-gathering methods are selected, it is essential to delineate a timeline for the evaluation project. The timeline should indicate specific dates by which each step is to be completed. Further, the schedule of evaluation activities should be made available to all those who will be affected by the activities. This dissemination of information is important not only for the timeline, but also for all of the other preliminary evaluation activities as well (i.e., identifying the evaluator, the purposes of the evaluation, and the evaluation questions and procedures). The smooth conduct of an evaluation depends on providing complete information to everyone involved.

Data Gathering

Once data-gathering instruments have been

selected or developed, and once timelines have been established, assessment instruments must be administered. While this step in the evaluation process seems straightforward, it does entail certain decisions. Those decisions may best be summarized in the questions Who?, What?, How?, Where?, and When?

First, who is to be interviewed or assessed—students, teachers, administrators, or parents? Are all of the representatives of each group to be dealt with, or only a portion? If only a portion, which representatives will be selected? Further, who will administer each of the assessment instruments? Will the project evaluator administer everything, or will the evaluator compile and analyze data resulting from administrations by others?

Second, what instrument is to be administered to whom? Recall that evaluators have at their disposal both formal tests and informal interviews for questions of language proficiency. In addition, there are questionnaires and interview questions for determining attitudes. Finally, observational checklists may be used to assess classroom interaction and instructional methodologies and activities.

Third, directly related to the assessment instrument chosen is the question of how it is administered. Again, what seems straightforward may mask certain points to be considered. For example, if students are to take a written test, how will directions be given: in a written format as well, or both orally and in writing? If interview questions are to be asked, how much explanation is allowed to be given ahead of time? If either students or teachers have questions, are they allowed to ask? If a formal oral test is given, may questions be repeated? If so, how many times may they be repeated? With respect to formal tests, whether oral or written, is there a time limit? Needless to say, the consistency of data-gathering procedures contributes to the reliability of the information collected.

Finally, the issue of consistency applies to the questions Where? and When? Where will tests and interviews be conducted—in the classroom, the hallway, the teachers' lounge? May questionnaires be taken home, or should they be completed at the site where they are distributed? <u>When</u> will assessments be made--on a given day or during a designated week? Will a morning test administration yield different results than an afternoon one? If an entire week is to be devoted to student assessment, which schools or grades will be examined first? For example, if several schools are involved, should all grades in one school be tested before all grades in another, or should all first grades be tested before all second grades, and so forth? Again, all of these questions need to be considered for the most effective data gathering.

Analysis and Interpretation

No evaluation study is complete, of course, without a compilation of the data collected and an interpretation of the results for future decision making. The procedures used for data compilation will be directly determined by the nature of the instruments used in gathering the data. On an attitude survey, for example, it may be stated that 85% of the respondents strongly agreed that foreign language study is essential for a well-rounded education, and that this result shows a 15% increase over the previous poll. In another example, it may be determined that the number of students scoring in the fourth quartile on a posttest of reading comprehension in German is significantly higher than the number on the pretest.
Once the data are compiled, they must be presented in an evaluation report, whether the report will serve as part of an ongoing evaluation or as a final report. Especially in the case of a final report, the document should consist of several sections: a description of the program and its goals, the questions and procedures of the evaluation, the results of the study, and an interpretation of the results, including programmatic implications (Bissell, 1980). This final section focusing on interpretations and implications of the data is the most important part of the evaluation. Data interpretation is essential for highlighting the strengths and weaknesses of

a program, as well as pinpointing possible explanations for those strengths and weaknesses. As in many situations, the data may be misleading without further analysis and discussion. As an example, it may be found in the evaluation of a second-grade FLES program that not a single student scored at the anticipated level of proficiency in a test of listening comprehension. Is the program ineffective then, and should it be discontinued? Or, after taking into consideration the fact that all students improved in listening comprehension from pretest scores, should it be concluded that the original program objective was set unrealistically high? Or further, after determining that only 5% of class time had been devoted to the development of listening skills, should one conclude that increased class time should be allotted for listening activities?

After the final report is written, it should, of course, be disseminated to the appropriate people. It is, perhaps, gratuitous to say that an evaluation report that is neither disseminated nor read serves no purpose; however, it is not uncommon for program reports to be ignored. Sometimes evaluation reports are skimmed only to ascertain whether a program is viewed, on the whole, as successful; details concerning recommendations for improvement may again be ignored. Given the time and money invested in program evaluation, it seems a double waste of resources when such lack of attention occurs.

SUMMARY

Both the goals of a given early foreign language program and the purposes for which an evaluation is intended will determine the nature of the evaluation design. However, a school district that wishes to collect the most meaningful data possible should make every effort to use a variety of approaches in assessing the effectiveness of a program. When feasible, for example, both short-term and long-term studies should be designed; both formative and sum-

mative evaluations should be considered. Both
product- and process-oriented evaluation questions
should be asked. Finally, a variety of data-gathering
tools should be used.

In addition, all those who are potentially or
actually affected by the evaluation must be informed
at all stages of the process. Such a dissemination of
information may not only facilitate the evaluation
process, but also lead to a receptive response to the
results. Finally, from a broader perspective, it must
be noted that an adequate number of seriously conducted evaluations will improve the overall quality of
early foreign language programs in the United States.

Readers who seek further information on program
evaluation may wish to consult Alkin, Daillak, and
White (1979); Morris, Fitz-Gibbon, and Henerson
(1978); Wilson (1977); and Walberg (1974). Those who
wish to pursue issues of language testing in general
are directed to the American Council on the Teaching
of Foreign Languages Provisional Proficiency Guidelines (ACTFL, 1982); Valette (1977); Oller (1983); and
Oller and Perkins (1980).

Chapter 6
Future Directions

AREAS OF NEED

As with any field of endeavor, the current state of the art is never wholly satisfactory to its practitioners. This statement is certainly applicable to the field of early foreign language study. While more is known now than in the past about second language acquisition, about the efficacy of particular methodologies and program types, and about appropriate evaluation procedures, there is no doubt that advances are necessary in a number of areas of early foreign language instruction. Among the numerous areas in need of further development, four major ones will be discussed here: the need for appropriate language assessment tools, for the establishment of an information clearinghouse, for an improved public relations system, and for continued research.

Assessment Tools

Since the determination of the effectiveness of a given early foreign language program generally depends on the levels of language proficiency attained by the students, it is obvious that valid and reliable language assessment instruments are essential. Unfortunately, such instruments are not readily available. In order for this situation to be rectified, two issues--one specific to early foreign language testing and one related to foreign language testing in general--must be considered.

First, there is the issue of tests appropriate for the chronological age and level of cognitive development of early foreign language students. While certain nationally normed and standardized foreign language tests are available for university students, such is not the case for elementary school students. Related to the issue of age-appropriate tests is that of program-appropriate tests. Once age-appropriate tests are devised, they need to be adjusted to suit the specific type of early foreign language program being studied. For example, given the more ambitious proficiency goals of a total immersion program, an instrument that is devised to assess the proficiency levels of third-grade immersion students would be inappropriately difficult for third-grade FLEX students.

In addition to the issue of age appropriateness, there is the major problem in language testing today of how global knowledge in a foreign language may best be assessed. Certainly, it is a relatively simple matter to develop discrete-point tests, that is, instruments that assess a person's knowledge of the discrete points of a language, such as the formation of plurals or the conjugations of verbs. However, since it is recognized that communicative effectiveness in a second language consists of much more than knowledge of discrete facts about the language, instruments need to be developed that can adequately assess a person's global knowledge. Clearly, much research is needed in the field of language testing in general before early foreign language programs can reap the benefits.

Information Clearinghouse

While this monograph and other documents like it may go some way toward meeting the information needs of those interested in early foreign language programs, there is a continuing need for a network or a clearinghouse to make information more readily available. Ideally, a separate clearinghouse could be established for the purposes of collecting and disseminating information specifically on early foreign language programs. Such a clearinghouse could be based at a university whose foreign language departments were interested in pedagogical issues.

Realistically speaking, the proposed clearing-house could be more readily established if it were incorporated into an already existing educational clearinghouse or research agency. In essence, the Center for Applied Linguistics has been unofficially serving in this capacity in recent years by virtue of its research projects and its monographs and news-letter articles devoted to early foreign language education. Further effort, however, is needed to facilitate the systematic collection of data from existing programs and the dissemination of information to educators who wish to refine or develop programs.

Public Relations

No matter how effective a given early foreign language program may be, its purposes and achievements may be ignored or misunderstood unless attention is paid to public relations matters. Such is certainly the case for any innovative educational program, not just early foreign language programs. With respect to public relations, three audiences should be kept in mind: teachers and administrators, parents and com-munity members in general, and educators at the state and national levels. Each target audience suggests a different mode for communicating information.

First of all, teachers and administrators in the school in which the program is housed need to be informed of the program's existence, its goals, and its ongoing activities. All too frequently, innova-tive educational programs are viewed with suspicion or have unrealistically high expectations placed on them --generally as the result of a lack of knowledge about the program. One way in which information about a program may be shared with teachers and administrators is to give a brief presentation at a faculty meeting or during an inservice day; regardless of the length of the presentation, time should be left for questions and comments. Another way of "advertising" a program's activities is to include brief, periodic announcements in school bulletins. Finally, bulletin board displays and student participation in school performances (e.g., a group of FLEX students singing a French song for the school's talent day) increase program visibility and, it is hoped, support for the program. Just as it is important to keep teachers and administrators in the home school informed about the program, it is also desirable to keep district personnel in other schools abreast of program developments. Educators need to be aware of educational activities in their district, especially if those activities are innovative and successful.

The next target audience to consider for public relations work consists of parents and other community members. Parents need to know the nature of the educational programs in which their children are participating so that they have appropriate expectations and offer appropriate support. Possible vehicles for delivering information to parents include presentations at parent-teacher meetings and newsletters from the program or school. In addition, parental visits to foreign language classes may be encouraged, as well as parental attendance at school performances involving foreign language students. Finally, students may be encouraged to bring their foreign language work home, especially when the work involves a special project or activity.

In addition to informing parents, program officials should see to it that community members in general are aware of the existence of an early foreign language program in their public schools. An occasional newspaper article, especially one with photographs, is the most common way to reach the community with a description of the program. In addition, program personnel in certain cities may wish to consider collaborating with a local cable television station on a program highlighting the early foreign language program. Finally, students' projects on the cathedrals of France or the folk arts of Mexico, to name two examples, could be displayed at local banks or shopping centers. All of these suggestions may serve to enhance the visibility of the early foreign language program in the community and, it is hoped, to increase public support for the program.

The final audience to consider for dissemination of information comprises other foreign language educators and school administrators at the state and national levels. Avenues available for the publication of information include professional newsletters and journals. In addition, educational conferences, both state and national, offer numerous opportunities for formal presentations, panel discussions, and "rap sessions." As already suggested by the recommendation of a clearinghouse, the sharing of information is essential for the advancement of the field of early foreign language education as a whole.

Research

The future of any educational approach depends heavily on the availability of research evidence demonstrating its effectiveness. Certainly the fields of second language acquisition in general and early foreign language education in particular are laden with research questions in need of answering. In addition to the programmatic questions already raised at the end of Chapter 3, much still needs to be learned about the process of second language acquisition. For example, how much input is sufficient to achieve optimal input? Does input that is not grammatically sequenced facilitate learning for all students? What are the salient characteristics of negotiated interaction? If a silent period is desirable, is there an optimal length? The answers to these and other research questions may help those involved in early foreign language education to make informed decisions about program type, methodologies, and materials.

SUMMARY

The viability and vitality of early foreign language education in the United States rely on the quality of programs currently in existence, as well as

on the future directions of the field. It is imperative that adequate and appropriate language assessment
instruments be developed, and that research on second
language acquisition and on the effectiveness of
programmatic approaches be continued. In addition,
the establishment of a clearinghouse is desirable for
the collection and dissemination of information on
early foreign language programs. Finally, public
relations work is essential for ensuring continued
support of these educational efforts.

•   •   •

Concluding Remarks

Any state-of-the-art discussion is, at best,
presumptuous and, at worst, ill-fated. On the one
hand, comprehensiveness is never fully attainable.
On the other hand, no sooner are statements made about
"current" second language acquisition theory and
research results, than they are contradicted by new
beliefs and findings. These limitations notwithstand-
ing, it is hoped that this monograph will serve
several purposes for educators interested in early
foreign language programs.
    First, the discussion of the rationale for early
foreign language study, coupled with information on
program types and research evidence of their effectiveness, may assist parents and educators in deciding
whether to establish a program and what form the
program should take if established. Next, the presentation of steps involved in the implementation and
evaluation processes may serve as a checklist for
district personnel. As a result, it is hoped that the
most common pitfalls in these two processes will be
avoided. Finally, the section on future directions
may remind educators of the current limitations as
well as the future possibilities of the field. With
well-informed decision makers in charge, the future of
foreign language in the elementary schools in the
United States may certainly be a promising one!

Chapter 7   Resources

BIBLIOGRAPHY

Note: *Asterisks indicate works that are cited in the text.*

Abramson, L.S., Abramson, D.A., Guerra, E.L., &
    Bristow, W.H. (1966). Hebrew in the elementary
    school. Brooklyn: Board of Education of the
    City of New York. (ERIC Document Reproduction
    Service No. ED 033 638)
Adams, L.S. (1967). If FLES is to succeed. National
    Education Association Journal, 56(9), 72.
Adams, M.S. (1972). The acquisition of academic
    skills and a second language through a program
    of total immersion. Unpublished master's thesis,
    University of California-Los Angeles.
Adcock, D.A. (1980). A comparison of the effects of
    three approaches upon the development of
    listening comprehension in Spanish and upon the
    improvement of reading skills in English of
    below-average readers enrolled in the first year
    of FLES Spanish (Grade 4) (Doctoral dissertation,
    The Ohio State University, 1980). Dissertation
    Abstracts International, 41/07-A, 2975. (Order
    No. DDJ81-00101)
Adiv, E. (1979). A comparison of early immersion and
    classes d'acceuil programs at the kindergarten
    level. Unpublished manuscript. Montreal,
    Quebec: Quebec Dept. of Education, Protestant
    School Board of Montreal. (ERIC Document
    Reproduction Service No. ED 225 372)

Adiv, E. (1980). An analysis of second language performance in two types of immersion programs (Doctoral dissertation, McGill University, Montreal, 1980). Dissertation Abstracts International, 41/03-A, 970.

Adiv, E. (1980). Starting French in kindergarten: The effects of program, mother tongue and other linguistic experience on second language development. Unpublished manuscript. Montreal, Quebec: Quebec Dept. of Education, Protestant School Board of Montreal. (ERIC Document Reproduction Service No. ED 225 368)

Adiv, E. (1981, March). Some observations on the nature of language transfer in the simultaneous acquisition of two second languages. Paper presented at the 9th Conference on Applied Linguistics, Ann Arbor, MI. (ERIC Document Reproduction Service No. ED 225 370)

*Alkin, M., Daillak, R., & White, P. (1979). Using evaluations: Does evaluation make a difference? Beverly Hills, CA: Sage Publications.

Allen, E.M. (1966). Foreign language below ninth grade: What are we doing? Modern Language Journal, 50, 101-104.

Allen, V.G. (1969). A book list to be used with French classes in the elementary school. Foreign Language Annals, 2, 336-42.

Allen, V.G. (1978). Foreign languages in the elementary school: A new look; a new focus. Language Arts, 55(2), 146-49.

*American Council on the Teaching of Foreign Languages. (1982). ACTFL provisional proficiency guidelines. Hastings-on-Hudson, NY: Author.

Anderson, H.H. (1984, March). The immersion approach: Principle and practice. Paper presented at the University of Wisconsin-Milwaukee's Linguistics Symposium on Current Approaches to Second Language Acquisition, Milwaukee. (ERIC Document Reproduction Service No. ED 245 527)

Anderson, H.H., & Rhodes, N.C. (1984). Immersion and other innovations in U.S. elementary schools. In S.J. Savignon & M.S. Barns (Eds.), Initiatives in communicative language teaching: A book of readings. Reading, MA: Addison-Wesley.

Andersson, T. (1961). Languages and education--A
    criticism. The Graduate Journal, 4(2), 406-421.
*Andersson, T. (1969). Foreign languages in the
    elementary school: A struggle against medioc-
    rity. Austin: University of Texas Press.
Andersson, T. (1981a). A guide to family reading in
    two languages: The preschool years. Rosslyn,
    VA: National Clearinghouse for Bilingual Educa-
    tion. (ERIC Document Reproduction Service No. ED
    215 560)
Andersson, T. (1981b). (Review of Second languages
    in primary education.) Modern Language Journal,
    65, 204.
Arendt, J.D. (1967). The role of FLES in developing
    skills for vocational and economic competence.
    In R.A. Pillet (Ed.), FLES and the objectives of
    the contemporary elementary schools (Report of
    the FLES Committee of the American Association of
    Teachers of French). Philadelphia, PA: Chilton.
    (ERIC Document Reproduction Service No. ED 081
    293)
Armada, F.R. (1978). A curriculum guide for Spanish
    foreign language on the elementary school level
    (Doctoral dissertation, District of Columbia
    Teachers College, 1978). Dissertation Abstracts
    International, 39/05-A, 2715. (Order No.
    DDJ78-21807)
*Asher, J. (1972). Children's first language as a
    model for second language learning. Modern Lan-
    guage Journal, 56, 133-39.
*Asher, J. (1977). Children learning another lan-
    guage. Child Development, 48, 1040-48.
*Asher, J. (1979). Learning another language through
    actions: The complete teacher's guidebook. Los
    Gatos, CA: Sky Oak Productions.
*Asher, J., & García, R. (1969). The optimal age to
    learn a foreign language. Modern Language Jour-
    nal, 53, 334-41.
*Asher, J., Kusudo, J., & de la Torre, R. (1974).
    Learning a second language through commands: The
    second field test. Modern Language Journal, 58,
    24-32.

Aspel, P. (1969). Wednesday, 10:00 A.M., a 1987 report on French in the elementary school. In G. Lipton (Ed.), FLES: Projections into the future (Report of the FLES committee of the American Association of Teachers of French). Boston: AATF. (ERIC Document Reproduction Service No. ED 077 302)

Aspel, P. (1970). Common goals of FLES and anthropology. In G. Lipton & V. Spaar-Rauch (Eds.), FLES patterns for change (Report of the FLES Committee of the American Association of Teachers of French). New Orleans: AATF. (ERIC Document Reproduction Service No. ED 077 302)

*Bagg, G.C., Oates, M.D., & Zucker, G.K. (1984). Building community support through a Spanish FLES program. Hispania, 67, 105-8.

*Baranick, W.A. (1985). The attitude of public elementary school principals towards second language acquisition programs in the elementary school. Unpublished doctoral dissertation, University of Maryland, College Park.

Barber, M.N. (1964). Provisions for articulation in foreign language programs in elementary and secondary schools (Doctoral dissertation, The Catholic University of America, 1964). Dissertation Abstracts International, 25/05, 2810. (Order No. 64-11077)

Bardin, J.A. (1966). French for elementary schools: A teaching guide. Albany, NY: State Education Department, Bureau of Elementary Curriculum Development. (ERIC Document Reproduction Service No. ED 010 729)

Barik, H.C., & Swain, M. (1975). Three-year evaluation of a large scale early grade French immersion program: The Ottawa study. Language Learning, 25(1), 1-30.

*Barik, H.C., & Swain, M. (1976). A Canadian experiment in bilingual education: The Peel study. Foreign Language Annals, 9, 465-79.

*Barik, H.C., & Swain, M. (1977). Report to the Elgin County board of education re: evaluation of the 1976-77 partial French immersion program in grades 5-7. Unpublished manuscript, Ontario

Institute for Studies in Education, Toronto,
Ontario.

*Barik, H.C., & Swain, M. (1978). Evaluation of a
bilingual education program in Canada: The Elgin
study through grade six. CILA Bulletin, 27,
32-58. (ERIC Document Reproduction Service No.
ED 174 043)

*Barik, H.C., Swain, M., & Gaudino, V. (1976). A
Canadian experiment in bilingual education in the
senior grades: The Peel study through grade ten.
International Review of Applied Psychology, 25,
99-113.

*Barik, H.C., Swain, M., & Nwanunobi, E. (1977).
English-French bilingual education: The Elgin
study through grade five. Canadian Modern Language Review, 33, 459-75.

Barnett, H. (1970). Let's harness FLES enthusiasm.
Hispania, 53, 979-82.

Barnett, H. (1973). Peer teaching: FLES program.
Hispania, 56, 635-38.

Bates, E.A. (1965). A report on the status of FLES
instruction in Texas. Hispania, 48, 122-24.

Baughin, J.A. (1983). A successful French weekend
camp. In Snyder, B. (Ed.), Speak out and touch
someone. The OMLTA Yearbook. Columbus, OH:
Ohio Modern Language Teacher's Association.
(ERIC Document Reproduction Service No. ED 230
055)

Benderson, A. (1983). Foreign languages in the
schools [Special issue]. Focus, 12. (ERIC
Document Reproduction Service No. ED 239 516)

Bendon, B.H. (1972). Useful current materials for
ESL, FLES, and bilingual classes. Instructor,
81(7), 36-37.

Bennett, R. (1975). Individualizing instruction
(FLES) with word games. Hispania, 58, 124-25.

Berman, J.H. (1982). Some effects of formal instruction on the attitudes and second language oral
proficiency of students enrolled in an early
total immersion program (Doctoral dissertation,
University of California-Los Angeles, 1982).
Dissertation Abstracts International, 43/06-A,
1861. (Order No. DDJ82-25572)

Birckbichler, D.W., & Muyskens, J.A. (1980). A
    personalized approach to the teaching of litera-
    ture at the elementary and intermediate levels of
    instruction. Foreign Language Annals, 13, 23-27.
Birkmaier, E.M. (1973). International understanding
    begins at home. In K. Jankowsky (Ed.), Language
    and international studies (Georgetown University
    Roundtable). Washington, DC: Georgetown
    University Press.
Bishop, R.H. (1966). Foreign language in the elemen-
    tary school: A study of methods in selected
    areas of Oregon (Doctoral dissertation, Univer-
    sity of Oregon, 1966). Dissertation Abstracts
    International, 27/07-A, 2093. (Order No.
    66-12952)
Bishop, R.H. (1980). The integrated story: Helping
    to take foreignness out of foreign language
    learning. Hispania, 63, 93-95.
*Bissell, J. (1980). Program impact evaluations: An
    introduction for managers of Title VII projects.
    Los Alamitos, CA: Southwest Research Laboratory
    Educational Research and Development.
Bonyun, R. (1982, December). Does a late immersion
    program make a difference to the graduates?
    Paper presented at the annual conference of the
    Ontario Educational Research Council, Toronto,
    Ontario. (ERIC Document Reproduction Service No.
    ED 233 595)
Bordie, J.G. (1971). When should instruction in a
    second language or dialect begin? FLES instruc-
    tion. Elementary English, 48, 551-58.
Bourque, E.H. (Ed.). (1968). The FLES student: A
    study (Report of 1967 FLES Committee of American
    Association of Teachers of French). Philadel-
    phia, PA: Chilton. (ERIC Document Reproduction
    Service No. ED 081 289)
Bourque, E.H. (1970). FLES is very much alive in
    Fairfield. Hispania, 53, 82-85.
Bourque, E.H. (1971). FLES: How to start a program.
    Instructor, 81(1), 146.
*Boyd, P. (1974). The acquisition of Spanish as a
    second language by Anglo children in the third
    year of an immersion program. Unpublished

master's thesis, University of California-Los
Angeles.

Brady, A.M., & Ruiz, F.H. (1967). Spanish FLES and
the AATSP. Hispania, 50, 872-74.

*Brega, E., & Newell, J.M. (1965). Comparison of
performance by "FLES" program students and regular French III students on Modern Language
Association tests. The French Review, 39(3),
433-38.

Brega, E., & Newell, J.M. (1967). High school performance of FLES and non-FLES students. Modern
Language Journal, 51, 408-11.

Breunig, M. (1960). Foreign languages in the elemen-
tary schools of the United States, 1959-60. New
York: Modern Language Association. (ERIC
Document Reproduction Service No. ED 003 952)

Broadbent, R. (1973). Some consequences of following
an elementary school curriculum in a second language. Unpublished master's thesis, University
of California at Los Angeles.

*Brown, H.D. (1980). Principles of language learning
and teaching. Englewood Cliffs, NJ: Prentice-
Hall.

Brown, M.J. (1965). A FLES research and experimental
project. Hispania, 48, 890-94.

*Bruck, M. (1978). The suitability of early French
immersion programs for the language disabled
child. Canadian Modern Language Review, 34,
884-87.

*Bruck, M. (1979). Problems in early French immer-
sion programs. In B. Mlacak and E. Isabelle
(Eds.), So you want your child to learn French!
Ottawa, Ontario: Canadian Parents for French.
(In ERIC Document Reproduction Service No. ED 213
248)

Burette, R. (1966). Training and recruitment of FLES
teachers. French Review, 39, 761-62.

Burstall, C. (1970). French in the primary school:
Attitudes and achievement. Slough, UK: National
Foundation for Educational Research in England
and Wales.

Burstall, C. (1975). French in the primary school:
The British experiment. The Canadian Modern
Language Review, 31, 388-402.

Burstall, C., et al. (1974). Primary French in the balance. Slough, UK: National Foundation for Educational Research in England and Wales.

Busser, A.S. (1966). An experiment in the teaching of French. The Independent School Bulletin, 25(3), 67-70.

Caldwell, G., & Beusch, A. (1972). Wholeness in learning: A curriculum guide for foreign language programs in the middle grades. Dover, DE: Delaware State Dept. of Public Instruction; Highland Springs, VA: Henrico County School System; Baltimore, MD: Maryland State Dept. of Education. (ERIC Document Reproduction Service No. ED 076 068)

California State Advisory Committee on Foreign Languages. (1972). Foreign language framework for California public schools: Kindergarten through grade twelve. Sacramento, CA: California State Board of Education. (ERIC Document Reproduction Service No. ED 058 790)

*California State Department of Education. (1975). California evaluation improvement project. Sacramento, CA: Author.

*California State Department of Education, Office of Bilingual Bicultural Education. (1984). Studies on immersion education. A collection for United States educators. Sacramento, CA: Author. (ERIC Document Reproduction Service No. ED 239 509)

*Campbell, R.N. (1972). Bilingual education in Culver City. Workpapers in Teaching English as a Second Language, 6(12), 87-91. (ERIC Document Reproduction Service No. ED 083 838)

*Campbell, R.N. (1984). The immersion approach to foreign language teaching. In J. Lundin & D.P. Dolson (Eds.), Studies on immersion education: A collection for United States educators. Sacramento, CA: California Department of Education, Office of Bilingual Bicultural Education. (ERIC Document Reproduction Service No. ED 239 509)

Campbell, R.N., & Galván, J.L. (1980, August). Bilingual education, language immersion, and home

language maintenance. Paper presented at the
Early Childhood Education Forum: A Bilingual
Perspective, Austin, TX.

Campbell, R.N., Taylor, D.M., & Tucker, G.R. (1973).
Teachers' views of immersion type bilingual
programs: A Quebec example. Foreign Language
Annals, 7, 106-10.

Canadian Parents for French. (1985). How to be an
immersion parent (pamphlet). Ottawa, Ontario:
Author.

Carroll, J.B., & Sapon, S.M. (1967). Modern language
aptitude test--Elementary manual. New York:
Psychological Corp.

Carson, L.A. (1965). The status of foreign language
teaching at the elementary school level in the
state of California, 1960-1961. Unpublished doctoral dissertation, University of Southern California, Los Angeles.

Castle, P. (1968). Successful FLES programs can be
achieved. In P. Castle & C. Jay (Eds.), Toward
excellence in foreign language education.
Springfield, IL; Illinois State Office of the
Superintendent of Public Instruction. (ERIC
Document Reproduction Service No. ED 034 448)

*Cathcart, R.L. (1972). Report on a group of Anglo
children after one year of immersion instruction
in Spanish. Unpublished master's thesis, University of California-Los Angeles.

*Chamot, A., & McKeon, D. (1984). Second language
teaching: An overview of methods. TESL
Reporter, 17, 63-66.

Chastain, K. (1980). Toward a philosophy of second-
language learning and teaching. Boston: Heinle
& Heinle.

Chestnut, D.T. (1969). Foreign language in the
elementary schools. Harrisburg, PA: Pennsylvania State Department of Public Instruction.
(ERIC Document Reproduction Service No. ED 037
143)

Chevalier, H.G. (1966). Let's teach German in the
grades. American School Board Journal, 153(2),
7.

*Chomsky, N. (1965). Aspects of the theory of syn-
tax. Cambridge, MA: MIT Press.

*Cincinnati Public Schools (see Curriculum Guides
     . . . next section)
*Cohen, A.D. (1974a). The Culver City Spanish immer-
     sion program: How does summer recess affect
     Spanish speaking ability? Language Learning,
     24(1), 55-68.
*Cohen, A.D. (1974b). The Culver City Spanish immer-
     sion program: The first two years. Modern Lan-
     guage Journal, 58, 95-103.
*Cohen, A.D. (1975a). A sociolinguistic approach to
     bilingual education. Rowley, MA: Newbury House.
Cohen, A.D. (1975b). Successful immersion education
     in North America. Working Papers in Bilingual-
     ism, 5. Toronto, Ontario: Ontario Institute for
     Studies in Education. (ERIC Document Reproduc-
     tion Service No. ED 125 241)
Cohen, A.D. (1976). The acquisition of Spanish
     grammar through immersion: Some findings after
     four years. Canadian Modern Language Review, 32,
     562-74.
Cohen, A.D. (1982). Researching the linguistic out-
     comes of bilingual programs. Bilingual Review,
     9(2), 97-108.
*Cohen, A.D., Fier, V., & Flores, M. (1973). The
     Culver City immersion program--End of year one
     and year two. Workpapers in Teaching English as
     a Second Language, 7, 65-74.
Cohen, A.D., & Swain, M. (1976). Bilingual educa-
     tion: The "immersion" model in the North
     American context. TESOL Quarterly, 10, 45-53.
The College Board. (1983). Academic preparation for
     college: What students need to know and be able
     to do. New York: Author. (ERIC Document
     Reproduction Service No. ED 232 517)
Cornfield, R.R. (1965). How much time for FLES?
     French Review, 39, 308-9.
Cornfield, R.R. (1966). The other side of FLES.
     Hispania, 49, 495-97.
Couture, L. (1969a). French in the Birmingham
     (Michigan) elementary schools. Foreign Language
     Annals, 2, 328-35.
*Cummins, J. (1976). The influence of bilingualism
     and cognitive growth: A synthesis of research

findings and explanatory hypotheses. <u>Working Papers on Bilingualism</u>, <u>9</u>, 1-43.

*Cummins, J. (1980). The entry and exit fallacy in bilingual education. <u>NABE Journal</u>, <u>4</u>(3), 25-59.

Cummins, J. (1981). Four misconceptions about language proficiency in bilingual education. <u>NABE Journal</u>, <u>5</u>(3), 31-45.

Cummins, J. (1983). Language proficiency, biliteracy and French immersion. <u>Canadian Journal of Education</u>, <u>8</u>, 117-38.

*Curran, C. (1976). <u>Counseling-learning in second languages</u>. Apple River, IL: Apple River Press.

Curtiss, M.L., & Curtiss, A. (1966). Modern languages in the grades: A questionnaire for school boards. <u>American School Board Journal</u>, <u>152</u>(3), 5-7.

Cziko, G.A. (1982). <u>Approaches to the evaluation of bilingual education: An international perspective</u> (Professional Papers, CZ-1). Los Alamitos, CA: National Center for Bilingual Research. (ERIC Document Reproduction Service No. ED 222 074)

Cziko, G.A., Holobow, N., & Lambert, W.E. (1977). <u>Early and late French immersion: A comparison of children at grade seven</u>. Unpublished manuscript, McGill University, Montreal, Quebec. (ERIC Document Reproduction Service No. ED 153 461)

*Cziko, G.A., Lambert, W., & Gutter, R. (1979). French immersion programs and students' social attitudes: A multidimensional investigation. <u>Working Papers on Bilingualism</u>, <u>19</u>, 13-28.

Cziko, G.A., Lambert, W.E., Sidoti, N., & Tucker, G.R. (1978). <u>Graduates of early immersion: Retrospective views of grade eleven students and their parents</u>. Unpublished manuscript, McGill University, Montreal, Quebec. (ERIC Document Reproduction Service No. ED 153 462)

Dammer, P.E., Glaude, P.M., & Green, J.R. (1968). FLES: A guide for program review. <u>Modern Language Journal</u>, <u>52</u>, 16-23.

Davenport, L.Y. (1978, October). <u>Elementary school: The optimum time for foreign language learning</u>. Paper presented at the joint conference of the

Southern Conference on Language Teaching and the
Texas Foreign Language Association, San Antonio,
TX. (ERIC Document Reproduction Service No. ED
168 301)

D.C. Public Schools, Division of Planning, Research,
and Evaluation. (1971). A study of the effect
of Latin instruction on English reading skills
of 6th grade students in the public schools of
the District of Columbia, school year 1970-71.
Washington, DC: Author. (ERIC Document
Reproduction Service No. ED 060 695)

De Lorenzo, W.E., & Gladstein, L.A. (1984). Immersion education à l'Americaine: A descriptive
study of U.S. immersion programs. Foreign Language Annals, 17, 35-40.

del Olmo, F.P., & del Olmo, G. (1967). FLES programs. NEA Journal, 56(5), 42-43.

Derrick, W., & Randeria, K. (1979). Early immersion
in French. Today's Education, 68(1), 38-40.

DiPietro, R. (1979). Filling the elementary curriculum with languages: What are the effects?
Modern Language Journal, 63, 192-201.

Donoghue, M.R. (1965a). Middle school grades are
best for starting a foreign language. The
Nation's Schools, 75(3), 74.

Donoghue, M.R. (1965b). A rationale for FLES.
French Review, 38, 523-29.

Donoghue, M.R. (1965c). Some states codes of FLES.
Modern Language Journal, 49, 358-60.

Donoghue, M.R. (1965d). What research tells us about
the effects of FLES. Hispania, 48, 555-58.

Donoghue, M.R. (1967). A rationale for FLES. In
M.R. Donoghue (Ed.), Foreign languages and the
schools: A book of readings. Dubuque, IA:
Brown.

Donoghue, M. (1968a). Foreign languages and the
elementary school child. Dubuque, IA: Brown.

Donoghue, M.R. (1968b). How second-language learning
differs from first-language learning. Hispania,
51, 480-81.

Donoghue, M.R. (1968c). The most critical problem in
FLES. The French Review, 42, 86-89.

Donoghue, M.R. (1969). Foreign languages in the
elementary school: Effects and instructional

arrangements according to research. ERIC Focus
Reports on the Teaching of Foreign Languages, 3.
New York: American Council on the Teaching of
Foreign Languages/Modern Language Association/
ERIC Clearinghouse on the Teaching of Foreign
Languages. (ERIC Document Reproduction Service
No. ED 031 979)

Donoghue, M.R. (1973). FLES and international understanding. Hispania, 56, 1059-65.

Donoghue, M.R. (1965a). Middle school grades are
best for starting a foreign language. The
Nation's Schools, 75(3), 74.

Donoghue, M.R. (1965b). Rationale for FLES. French
Review, 38, 523-29.

Donoghue, M.R. (1965c). Some states codes of FLES.
Modern Language Journal, 49, 358-60.

Donoghue, M.R. (1965d). What research tells us about
the effects of FLES. Hispania, 48, 555-58.

Donoghue, M.R. (1967). A rationale for FLES. In
M.R. Donoghue (Ed.), Foreign languages and the
schools: A book of readings. Dubuque, IA:
Brown.

Donoghue, M. (1968a). Foreign languages and the
elementary school child. Dubuque, IA: Brown.

Donoghue, M.R. (1968b). How second-language learning
differs from first-language learning. Hispania,
51, 480-81.

Donoghue, M.R. (1968c). The most critical problem in
FLES. The French Review, 42(1), 86-89.

Donoghue, M.R. (1969). Foreign languages in the
elementary school: Effects and instructional
arrangements according to research. ERIC Focus
Reports on the Teaching of Foreign Languages, 3.
New York: American Council on the Teaching of
Foreign Languages/Modern Language Association/
ERIC Clearinghouse on the Teaching of Foreign
Languages. (ERIC Document Reproduction Service
No. ED 031 979)

Donoghue, M.R. (1973). FLES and international understanding. Hispania, 56, 1059-65.

Donoghue, M.R. (1978). Presenting the cultural component during FLES. Hispania, 61, 124-26.

Donoghue, M.R. (1981). Recent research in FLES
(1975-80). Hispania, 64, 602-4.

Donoghue, M.R., & Kunkle, J.F. (1979). Second languages in primary education. Rowley, MA: Newbury House.

Dufort, M.R. (1962). The effect of two methods of FLES instruction on student audio comprehension (Doctoral dissertation, University of California, Berkeley, 1962). Dissertation Abstacts International, X1962, 93.

*Dulay, H., Burt, M., & Krashen, S. (1982). Language two. New York: Oxford University Press.

Durette, R.E. (1968). Pupil achievement in a normal FLES program compared with pupil achievement in an intensive program (Doctoral dissertation, Florida State University, 1968). Dissertation Abstracts International, 30/02-A, 515. (Order No. 69-13, 262)

Durette, R.E. (1972). A five year FLES report. Modern Language Journal, 56, 23-24.

Eddy, P.A. (1978). Does FL study aid native language development? ERIC/CLL News Bulletin, 2(2), 1-2.

Eddy, P.A. (1980a). Foreign language in the USA: A national survey of American attitudes and experience. Modern Language Journal, 64, 58-63. (In ERIC Document Reproduction Service No. ED 179 117)

Eddy, P.A. (1980b). Present status of foreign language teaching: A Northeast Conference survey. In T.H. Geno (Ed.), 1980 Reports of the Northeast Conference. Middlebury, VT: Northeast Conference. (In ERIC Document Reproduction Service No. ED 191 304)

Edwards, H.P., & Casserly, M.C. (1976). Research and evaluation of second language (French) programs in schools of the Ottawa Roman Catholic Separate School Board (Annual Reports 1971-1972 and 1972-1973). Ottawa, Ontario: University of Ottawa Press.

Edwards, H.P., & Smyth, F. (1976). Evaluation of second language programs and some alternatives for teaching French as a second language in grades five to eight. Ottawa, Ontario: University of Ottawa Press.

Eriksson, M., Forest, I., & Mulhauser, R. (1964).
  Foreign languages in the elementary school.
  Englewood Cliffs, NJ: Prentice-Hall.
*Ervin-Tripp, S. (1974). Is second language learning
  like the first? TESOL Quarterly, 8, 111-27.
*Fairfax County Public Schools (see Curriculum Guides
  . . . next section)
*Fathman, A.K. (1975). Language background, age and the
  order of acquisition of English structures. In
  M. Burt & H. Dulay (Eds.), New directions in
  second language learning, teaching and bilingual
  education. Washington, DC: TESOL.
Feitelson, D. (1976). Mother tongue or second lan-
  guage? On the teaching of reading in multilin-
  gual societies. Newark, DE: International
  Reading Association. (ERIC Document Reproduction
  Service No. ED 166 672)
Fernandez, L.B. (1973). The Spanish FLES picture in
  New York state. Hispania, 56, 111-14.
Fielstra, H.A.D. (1967). Relationship between
  selected factors and pupil success in elementary
  school foreign language classes (Doctoral disser-
  tation, Stanford University, 1967). Dissertation
  Abstracts International, 28/01-A, 153. (Order
  No. 67-07986)
Fier, V. (1974). The Culver City Spanish immersion
  program: An overview. Unpublished master's the-
  sis, Occidental College, Los Angeles, CA.
Fillmore, L.W. (1983). The language learner as an
  individual: Implications of research on individual differences for the ESL teacher. In M.A.
  Clarke & J. Handscombe (Eds.), On TESOL '82:
  Pacific perspectives on language learning and
  teaching: III. Conditions for learning. Wash-
  ington, DC: Teachers of English to Speakers of
  Other Languages. (ERIC Document Reproduction
  Service No. ED 228 893)
Fink, A.W., & Lightfoot, Y. (1967). Pasadena's
  foreign language program for children in the ele-
  mentary schools. In M.R. Donoghue (Comp.),
  Foreign languages and the schools: Book of
  readings. Dubuque, IA: Brown.
Fischer, W. (1971). FLES and grass roots education.
  In Reports from the 1971 annual meeting of the

Washington Association of Foreign Language
Teachers. Pullman, WA: WAFLT. (ERIC Document
Reproduction Service No. ED 052 645)

Fischer, W. (1972, March). Is FLES holding its own?
Paper presented at the Pacific Northwest State
Conference of Foreign Languages, Spokane, WA.

Fisk, S. (1969). What goals for FLES? Hispania, 52,
64-69.

Flores, M. (1973). An early stage in the acquisition
of Spanish morphology by a group of English-
speaking children. Unpublished master's thesis,
University of California-Los Angeles.

Ford, J.F. (1974). FLES methods: A proposed course
syllabus. Hispania, 57, 301-4.

Fryer, T.B. (1970). Toward a systems approach in the
preparation of elementary foreign language teachers: A description of overt teacher behaviors in
the area of professional preparation as perceived
by foreign language teachers (Doctoral dissertation, University of Texas, 1970). Dissertation
Abstracts International, 31/11-1, 5904. (Order
No. 71-11536)

Fryer, T.B., & Michel, J. (1970). FLES certification: A lack of progress report. Hispania, 53,
460-464.

Galante, V.V. (1967). Don't try FLES unless you can
follow this recipe. Instructor, 76(8), 100-101.

Galante, V.V. (1970). FLES, Hicksville, N.Y.:
Another decade of success. Hispania, 53, 464-65.

Galas, E.M. (1969). The development and evaluation
of an elementary school foreign language teaching
technique for use by teachers with inadequate
knowledge of the language taught (Doctoral
dissertation, University of Michigan, 1969).
Dissertation Abstracts International, 28/07-A,
2820. (Order No. 66-11,799)

*Galván, J.L. (1978, April). A progress report on
the learning of Spanish by English speakers in
the Culver City immersion program: Spanish
reading. Paper presented at the annual meeting
of Teachers of English to Speakers of Other Languages, Mexico City.

Galván, J.L., & Campbell, R. (1979). An examination
of the communication strategies of two children

in the Culver City Spanish immersion program. In
R.W. Andersen (Ed.), The acquisition and use of
Spanish and English as first and second lan-
guages. Washington, DC: Teachers of English to
Speakers of Other Languages.

Galván, J.L., Imamura, A., & Jaffe, B. (1977, Novem-
ber). A report on research in progress in the
Culver City Spanish immersion program. Paper
presented at the annual meeting of the American
Council of Teachers of Foreign Languages, San
Francisco.

*García, M., & Grady, K. (1984, April). Summer HILT
experience: ESL and SSL for elementary school.
Paper presented at the annual meeting of the
California Association of Teachers of English to
Speakers of Other Languages, San Jose. (ERIC
Document Reproduction Service No. ED 245 552)

Garibaldi, V.B. (1968). The development of a broader
rationale for foreign languages in the elementary
schools and guidelines for its implementation
(Doctoral dissertation, Ohio State University,
1968). Dissertation Abstracts International,
29/05-A, 1361. (Order No. 68-15319)

Gaskell, W.G. (1967). They dropped the ball on FLES.
Modern Language Journal, 51, 79-81.

*Gattegno, C. (1972). Teaching foreign languages in
schools: The silent way. New York: Educational
Solutions. (ERIC Document Reproduction Service
No. ED 157 403)

*Genesee, F. (1974). An evaluation of the English
writing skills of students in French immersion
programs. Unpublished manuscript, Protestant
School Board of Greater Montreal.

*Genesee, F. (1976). The role of intelligence in
second language learning. Language Learning, 26,
267-80.

*Genesee, F. (1978a). Is there an optimal age for
starting second language instruction? McGill
Journal of Education, 13(2), 145-54. (ERIC
Document Reproduction Service No. ED 182 992)

*Genesee, F. (1978b). A longitudinal evaluation of
an early immersion school program. Canadian
Journal of Education, 3, 31-50.

Genesee, F. (1979). Scholastic effects of French immersion: An overview after ten years. Inter-change on Educational Policy, 9(4), 20-29.

Genesee, F. (1983). Bilingual education of majority-language children: The immersion experiments in review. Applied Psycholinguistics, 4, 1-46.

*Genesee, F. (1984). Historical and theoretical foundations of immersion education. In Lundin, J., & Dolson, D.P. (Eds.), Studies on immersion education: A collection for United States educators. Sacramento, CA: California Department of Education, Office of Bilingual Bicultural Education. (ERIC Document Reproduction Service No. ED 239 509)

*Genesee, F., & Lambert, W. (1983). Trilingual education for majority language children. Child Development, 54, 105-14.

*Genesee, F., Polich, E., & Stanley, M. (1977). An experimental French immersion program at the secondary school level 1969 to 1974. Canadian Modern Language Review, 33, 318-32.

*Genesee, F., Tucker, G.R., & Lambert, W. (1975). Communication skills of bilingual children. Child Development, 46, 1010-14.

Georgeoff, J. (1971). Research in FLES 1961-1970. American Foreign Language Teacher, 2(2), 27-31, 44-45.

Georgeoff, J. (Comp). (1972). FLES bibliography. American Foreign Language Teacher, 2(3), 45-47.

Ginsburg, H.J., & McCoy, I.H. (1981). An empirical rationale for foreign languages in elementary schools. Modern Language Journal, 65, 36-42.

Gordon, F.N. (1981). Foreign languages for the gifted and talented. Harrisburg, PA: Pennsylvania Department of Education, Bureau of Curriculum Services.

Gradisnik, A. (1966). Television can be effective in the FLES program ... If. Hispania, 49(3), 485-89.

Gradisnik, A. (1968). A survey of FLES instruction in cities over 300,000. Foreign Language Annals, 2, 54-57.

*Gray, T., Rhodes, N., Campbell, R., & Snow, M. (1984). Comparative evaluation of elementary

school foreign language programs. Final report.
Washington, DC: Center for Applied Linguistics.
(ERIC Document Reproduction Service No. ED 238
255)

Green, J. (1979). Hello, world! Instructor, 89(3),
91-94.

Grittner, F.M. (1974). Foreign languages and the
changing curriculum. NASSP Bulletin, 58(384),
71-78.

*Guiora, A., Brannon, R., & Dull, C. (1972). Empathy
and second language learning. Language Learning,
22, 111-30.

Gunther, W.J. (1966). A study of informed opinion
related to the television teacher of foreign languages in elementary schools (Doctoral dissertation, Rutgers University, The State University of
New Jersey-New Brunswick, 1966). Dissertation
Abstracts International, 27/06-A, 1544. (Order
No. 66-12072)

Hancock, C.R., Lipton, G.C., & Baslaw, A. (1976). A
study of FLES and non-FLES pupils' attitudes
towards the study of French. French Review, 49,
717-22.

*Harley, B. (1979). French gender rules in the
speech of English-dominant, French-dominant, and
monolingual French-speaking children. Working
Papers on Bilingualism, 19, 129-56.

*Harley, B. (1982). Age-related differences in the
acquisition of the French verb system by Anglo-
phone students in French immersion programs.
Unpublished doctoral dissertation, University of
Toronto, Ontario.

Harmon, J.T. (Ed.). (1965). A supplement for Spanish
and Portuguese to the 1962 Selective List of
Materials for use by teachers of modern foreign
languages in elementary and secondary schools.
New York: Modern Language Association of
America. (ERIC Document Reproduction Service No.
ED 020 705)

Hartlaub, E.F. (1961). Two methods of teaching
foreign language in selected elementary schools
(Doctoral dissertation, The Pennsylvania State
University, 1961). Dissertation Abstracts International, 22/11, 3948. (Order No. 62-01715)

Hauptman, P.C. (1971). A structural approach vs. a situational approach to foreign-language teaching. Language Learning, 21, 235-44.

Haydu, J. (1969). FLES and the pleasures of learning. Hispania, 52, 886-89.

Haynes, J.S. (1981). An analysis of change in attitude and communication skills of students participating in a weekend immersion program in foreign language (Doctoral dissertation, George Peabody College for Teachers, 1981). Dissertation Abstracts International, 42/06-A, 2470. (Order No. DDJ81-21579)

*Haynes, J. (1983). Weekend immersion in foreign language and culture. Educational Leadership, 40, 64.

Hilaire, M. (1966). Evaluation of the FLES movement. Catholic School Journal, vol?(no.?), 65-66.

Hornby, P.A. (1980). Achieving second language fluency through immersion education. Foreign Language Annals, 13, 107-13.

Howe, E.C. (1983). The success of the Cherry Hill Spanish immersion program in Orem, Utah. Hispania, 66, 592-97.

Hunter, M. (1974). Individualizing FLES. Hispania, 57, 494-97. (ERIC Document Reproduction Service No. ED 049 667)

*Indiana Dept. of Public Instruction (see Curriculum Guides . . . next section)

Irvine, D.J. (1977, March). Evaluation methodology for a French language immersion program. Paper presented at the Evaluation Workshop on the French Language Immersion Program, Plattsburgh, NY. (ERIC Document Reproduction Service No. ED 139 255)

Jackson, M.H. (1973). FLES? Yes! School and Community, 59(8), 27.

Jacobs, G.H.L. (1978). An American foreign language immersion program: How to. Foreign Language Annals, 11, 405-13. (ERIC Document Reproduction Service No. ED 159 919)

Jaffe, B. (1978). Strategies of communication: Spanish immersion program. Unpublished master's thesis, University of California-Los Angeles.

Jarvis, G.A. (Ed.). (1976). An integrative approach
    to foreign language teaching: Choosing among the
    options. Skokie, IL: National Textbook Co.
    (ERIC Document Reproduction Service No. ED 158
    561)
Jashni, V.M. (1976). The Effects of Spanish immer-
    sion program on the kindergarten-primary students
    in affective and cognitive domains. (Doctoral
    dissertation, Brigham Young University, 1976).
    Dissertation Abstracts International, 36/08-A,
    5019. (Order No. DDJ76-02562)
JeKenta, A.W., & Fearing, P. (1968). Current trends
    in curriculum: Elementary and secondary schools.
    In E.M. Birkmaier (Ed.), Britannica Review of
    Foreign Language Education (vol. 1). Chicago:
    Encyclopaedia Britannica.
Johnson, C.E., Flores, J.S., Ellison, F.P., & Riestra,
    M.A. (1964). The development and evaluation of
    methods and materials to facilitate foreign lan-
    guage instruction in elementary schools (Doctoral
    dissertation, University of Illinois at Urbana-
    Champaign, 1964). Dissertation Abstracts Inter-
    national, 28/07-A, 2821. (Order No. 64-13,941)
Johnson, C.E., Flores, J.S., Ellison, F.P., & Riestra,
    M.A. (1967). The non-specialist teacher in
    FLES. Modern Language Journal, 51, 76-79.
Johnston, M. (1968, August). FLES for everybody.
    Paper presented at the national convention of the
    American Association of Teachers of Spanish and
    Portuguese, San Antonio. (ERIC Document Repro-
    duction Service No. ED 030 341)
Jonas, R.A. (1966). FLES specialist teacher program.
    Modern Language Journal, 50, 492-93.
Jonas, R.A. (1969). The twinned classroom approach
    to FLES. Modern Language Journal, 53, 342-46.
*Karabinus, R. (1976). Report of foreign language
    instruction differences in grades 5, 6, and 7.
    Unpublished manuscript, Hinsdale Public
    Schools, Hinsdale, IL.
Keene, J., & Nolan, J. (1967). FLES: Does force
    feeding work? Schoolmen complain: Too little
    money and too much Spanish hurt California's com-
    pulsory grade school foreign language program.
    The Nation's Schools, 79(5), 79-84, 118.

Kennedy, D.F., & De Lorenzo, W.E. (1985). Complete guide to exploratory foreign language programs. Lincolnwood, IL: National Textbook Co.

Kerr, B. (Ed.). (1983). Colloquium on French as a second language: Proceedings. Review and Evaluation Bulletin, 4(4). (ERIC Document Reproduction Service No. ED 239 504)

*Kodjak, B., & Hayser, K. (1982, April). French for children: Aspects of an elementary school foreign language program. Paper presented at the Northeast Conference on the Teaching of Foreign Languages, New York. (ERIC Document Reproduction Service No. ED 223 067)

*Krashen, S.D. (1981). Second language acquisition and second language learning. Oxford, UK: Pergamon Press.

*Krashen, S.D. (1983). Principles and practice in second language acquisition. Oxford, UK: Pergamon Press.

Krashen, S.D., Long, M.A., & Scarcella, R.C. (1979). Age, rate, and eventual attainment in second language acquisition. TESOL Quarterly, 13, 573-82.

Krashen, S.D., Long, M.A., & Scarcella, R.C. (Eds.). (1982). Child-adult differences in second language acquisition. Rowley, MA: Newbury House.

*Krashen, S.D., & Terrell, T. (1983). The natural approach to language acquisition in the classroom. Oxford, UK: Pergamon Press; San Francisco: Alemany Press.

Kunkle, J.F. (1966). Two years with the Saint-Cloud materials. Modern Language Journal, 50, 137-39.

Kunkle, J.F. (1972). Now that FLES is dead, what next? Educational Leadership, 29, 417-19.

*Lalande, J.F. II, & Taylor, H.F. (1982). Planting the seed: German at the kindergarten level. Die Unterrichtspraxis, 15, 254-63.

*Lambert, W. (1984). An overview of issues in immersion education. In J. Lundin & D.P. Dolson (Eds.), Studies on immersion education: A collection for U.S. educators. Sacramento, CA: California State Department of Eduation. (ERIC Document Reproduction Service No. ED 239 509)

*Lambert, W.E., & Tucker, G.R. (1972). Bilingual
    education of children: The St. Lambert experi-
    ment. Rowley, MA: Newbury House.
Lambert, W.E., Tucker, G.R., & d'Anglejan, A. (1973).
    Cognitive and attitudinal consequences of bilin-
    gual schooling. The St. Lambert project through
    grade five. Journal of Educational Psychology,
    65, 141-59.
Landor, R.A. (1971). Foreign language in elementary
    liberal education. Modern Language Journal, 55,
    508-510.
Landry, R.G. (1973). The enhancement of figural
    creativity through second language learning at
    the elementary school level. Foreign Language
    Annals, 7, 111-15.
Landry, R.G. (1973). The relationship of second
    language learning and verbal creativity. Modern
    Language Journal, 57, 110-13.
Landry, R.G. (1974). A comparison of second language
    learners and monolinguals on divergent thinking
    tasks at the elementary school level. Modern
    Language Journal, 58(1-2), 10-15.
*Langer, S. (1958). Philosophy in a new key: A
    study in the symbolism of reason, rite, and art.
    New York: The New American Library.
*Lapkin, S. (1982). The English writing skills of
    French immersion pupils at grade five.
    Canadian Modern Language Review, 39, 24-33.
*Lapkin, S., & Cummins, J. (1984). Canadian French
    immersion education: Current administrative and
    instructional practices. In J. Lundin & D.P.
    Dolson (Eds.), Studies on immersion education:
    A collection for United States educators.
    Sacramento, CA: California State Department of
    Education. (ERIC Document Reproduction Service
    No. ED 239 509)
Larew, L.A. (1973). LAPS for FLES in individualized
    instruction. Hispania, 56, 114-16.
Larew, L.A. (1975). FLES in Puerto Rico--revisited.
    Hispania, 58, 122-24.
Larew, L.A. (1976). Reading readiness activities for
    FLES. Hispania, 59, 893-95.
*Lebach, S. (1974). A report on the Culver City
    Spanish Immersion Program in its third year: Its

implications for language and subject matter acquisition, language use, and attitudes. Unpublished master's thesis, University of California-Los Angeles. (ERIC Document Reproduction Service No. ED 129 104)

Lee, V. (1983, December). An interdisciplinary immersion program in foreign languages. Paper presented at the annual meeting of the Modern Language Association, New York. (ERIC Document Reproduction Service No. ED 240 851)

Lee, V. (1983). A new interdisciplinary program. ADFL Bulletin, 15(1), 4-6.

Lee, W.R. (1977). For and against an early start. Foreign Language Annals, 10, 263-70.

Leibowitz, S., & Sherman, D. (1966). FLES workshop. Instructor, 75(5), 131.

Leino, W.B., & Haak, L.A. (1963). The teaching of Spanish in the elementary schools and the effects on achievement in other selected subject areas. St. Paul, MN: St. Paul Public Schools. (ERIC Document Reproduction Service No. ED 001 301)

Levenson, S. (1965). Preparing for FLES--The study group approach. Modern Language Journal, 49, 94-96.

Levenson, S. (1966). Articulating FLES programs: A plan of action! Hispania, 49, 296-98.

Levenson, S., & Kendrick, W. (1967). Readings in foreign languages for the elementary schools. Waltham, MA: Blaisdell Publishing.

Lieblich, M.Z. (1963). Effectiveness of methods of teaching foreign language sounds: A comparative analysis of the effectiveness of methods in teaching the correct production of French language sounds to elementary school children (Doctoral dissertation, New York University, 1963). Dissertation Abstracts International, 24/04, 1749. (Order No. 63-06670)

Lipton, G.C. (1967). New trends in FLES: A quiet optimism. Hispania, 50, 122-24.

Lipton, G.C. (1969a). The effectiveness of listening-speaking-only, as compared with listening-speaking-reading in grade four. The first year of study of French at the FLES level, in the acquisition of auditory comprehension (Doctoral dissertation, New York University, 1969). <u>Dissertation Abstracts International</u>, 30/06-A, 2421. (Orde No. 69-21217)

Lipton, G.C. (Ed.). (1969b). <u>FLES: Projections into the future</u> (Report of the FLES Committee of the American Association of Teachers of French). Boston: American Association of Teachers of French. (ERIC Document Reproduction Service No. ED 077 304)

Lipton, G.C. (1969c). To read or not to read: An experiment on the FLES level. <u>Foreign Language Annals</u>, 3, 241-46.

Lipton, G.C. (Ed.). (1971). <u>Report of the FLES Committee of the American Association of Teachers of French</u>. Washington, DC: AATF.

*Lipton, G.C. (1979). <u>Yes to LEX, or elementary school foreign language instruction helps English language skills: Results of a pilot study</u>. Unpublished paper. (Available from author, Dept. of Modern Languages and Linguistics, Univ. of Maryland, Baltimore Co., Catonsville, MD 21228)

Lipton, G.C., & Bourque, E.H. (Eds.). (1969). <u>Research, relevance, and reality: The three R's of FLES</u>. Detroit: American Association of Teachers of French. (ERIC Document Reproduction Service No. ED 077 303)

Lipton, G.C., & Bourque, E.H. (Eds.). (1972). <u>FLES U.S.A. success stories</u> (Report by the FLES Committee of the American Association of Teachers of French). New York: American Association of Teachers of French. (ERIC Document Reproduction Service No. ED 093 150)

Lipton, G.C., & Spaar-Rauch, V. (Eds.). (1970). <u>FLES: Patterns for change</u> (Report by the FLES Committee of the American Association of Teachers of French). New Orleans: American Association of Teachers of French. (ERIC Document Reproduction Service No. ED 077 302)

Lipton, G.C., & Spaar-Rauch, V. (Eds.). (1971). <u>FLES: Goals and guides</u> (Report by the FLES Committee of the American Association of Teachers of French). New Orleans: American Association of Teachers of French. (ERIC Document Reproduction Service No. ED 093 149)

*Long, M.H. (1980). Input, interaction, and second
    language acquisition. (Doctoral dissertation,
    University of California at Los Angeles, 1980).
    Dissertation Abstracts International, 41/12-A,
    5082. (Order No DDJ81-11249)
*Long, M.H. (1981). Input, interaction, and second
    language acquisition. In H. Winitz (Ed.), Native
    Language and Foreign Language Acquisition (Annals
    of the New York Academy of Sciences, 379), pp.
    259-78.
Lopato, E. (1963). FLES and academic achievement.
    The French Review, 36(5), 499-507.
Love, F.W.D., & Honig, L.J. (1973). Options and per-
    spectives: A sourcebook of innovative foreign
    language programs in action, K-12. New York:
    American Council on the Teaching of Foreign
    Languages. (ERIC Document Reproduction Service
    No. ED 107 100)
*Lozanov, G. (1979). Suggestology and outlines of
    suggestopedy. New York: Gordon and Breach.
Lundin, J., & Dolson, D.P. (Eds.). (1984). Studies
    on immersion education: A collection for U.S.
    educators. Sacramento, CA: California State
    Dept. of Education, Office of Bilingual Bicul-
    tural Education. (ERIC Document Reproduction
    Service No. ED 239 509)
Macaulay, R. (1980). Generally speaking: How chil-
    dren learn language. Rowley, MA: Newbury House.
MacDonald, D. (1973). No less than FLES. American
    Foreign Language Teacher, 3(2), 9-11.
Mace, B.J. (1971). Should the objectives and the
    nature of a FLES program be changed to meet spe-
    cial needs? Hispania, 54, 498-99.
*Macnamara, J. (1975). Comparison between first and
    second language learning. Working Papers on
    Bilingualism, 7, 71-94.
Macwhinney, J.E. (1964). Administrative considera-
    tions applicable to foreign language programs in
    elementary schools (Doctoral dissertation, Uni-
    versity of Southern California, 1964). Disserta-
    tion Abstracts International, 25/06, 3360.
    (Order No. 64-12480)
Marjama, P. (1975). Success in a bilingual first
    grade. Hispania, 58, 330-32.

Masciantonio, R. (1974). A FLES Latin lesson--
     Philadelphia style. American Foreign Language
     Teacher, 4(3), 30-32.
Massachusetts Department of Education. (1976).
     Massachusetts educational assessment program.
     Foreign language 1975-1976. Boston, MA: Author.
     (ERIC Document Reproduction Service No. ED 201
     208)
Massey, D.A., & Potter, J. (1979). A bibliography of
     articles and books on bilingualism in education.
     Ottawa, Ontario: Canadian Parents for French.
Mavrogenes, N.A. (1977). The effect of elementary
     Latin instruction on language arts performance.
     The Elementary School Journal, 77, 268-73.
Mavrogenes, N.A. (1979). Latin in the elementary
     school: A help for reading and language arts.
     Classical Outlook, 57(2), 33-35.
*McEachern, W. (1980). Parental decision for French
     immersion: A look at some influencing factors.
     Canadian Modern Language Review, 38, 238-46.
McGillivray, W.R. (Ed.). (1986). More French, S'Il
     Vous Plait. Ottawa, Ontario: Canadian Parents
     for French.
McInnis, C.E., Burstall, C., Rivers, W.M., & Carrol,
     J.B. (1976). Three studies of experimental
     French programs and comments of guest analysts.
     Canadian Modern Language Review, 33(2), 151-61.
McInnis, C.E., & Donoghue, E.E. (1976). Research and
     evaluation of second language (French) programs.
     Toronto, Ontario: Ontario Department of
     Education.
McKee, E. (1983, March). The effects of intensive
     language instruction on student performance in
     beginning college French. Paper presented at the
     Central States Conference on the Teaching of
     Foreign Languages, St. Louis, MO. (ERIC Document
     Reproduction Service No. ED 233 601)
McKim, L.W. (1970). FLES: Types of programs (ERIC
     Focus Reports on the Teaching of Foreign Lan-
     guages, No. 16). New York: American Council on
     the Teaching of Foreign Languages. (ERIC Docu-
     ment Reproduction Service No. ED 043 268)

McKim, L.W. (1972). Quality foreign language instruction in the elementary schools. Hispania, 55, 500-506.

McLaughlin, B. (1978). Second-language acquisition in childhood. New York: Halsted Press.

*McLaughlin, B. (1982). Children's second language learning. Washington, DC: ERIC Clearinghouse on Languages and Linguistics. (ERIC Document Reproduction Service No. ED 217 701)

Mead, R.G., Jr. (Ed.). (1983). Foreign languages: Key links in the chain of learning. Middlebury, VT: Northeast Conference on the Teaching of Foreign Languages. (ERIC Document Reproduction Service No. ED 240 863)

Melaro, C.L. (1973). FLES report: Simplify for success. Instructor, 83(3), 53.

Met, M. (1978). Bilingual education for speakers of English. Foreign Language Annals, 11, 35-40.

Met, M. (1984). Immersion and the language minority student (Revised version). Milwaukee, WI: University of Wisconsin-Milwaukee, Midwest National Origin Desegregation Assistance Center. (ERIC Document Reproduction Service No. ED 240 835)

Met, M. (1980). The rebirth of foreign languages in the elementary schools. Educational Leadership, 37, 321-323.

Milwaukee Public Schools. (1981). Percentage of third-grade pupils scoring in three categories of the Distribution Metropolitan Achievement Tests. Unpublished manuscript.

*Milwaukee Public Schools (see Curriculum Guides . . . next section)

Mirsky, J. (1969). Overabundance of FLES. Hispania, 52, 259-63.

Mlacak, B., & Isabelle, E. (Eds.). (1979). So you want your child to learn French! A handbook for parents. Ottawa, Ontario: Canadian Parents for French.

Modern Language Association. (1954). Foreign languages in the elementary schools: Some questions and answers. New York: Author.

Modern Language Association. (1961). Foreign languages in the elementary schools: A second

statement of policy. New York: Author. (ERIC
Document Reproduction Service No. ED 019 906)

Moore, J.M. (1971). (Review of Foreign languages in
the elementary school: A struggle against
mediocrity). German Quarterly, 44, 113-116.

*Morris, L., FitzGibbon, C., & Henerson, M. (1978).
Program evaluation kit. Beverly Hills: Sage
Publications.

*Morrison, F., Bonyun, R., Pawley, C., & Walsh, M.
(1979). French proficiency status of Ottawa and
Carleton students in alternative programs: Evaluation of the second language learning (French)
programs in the schools of Ottawa and Carleton
Board of Education (Sixth annual report).
Toronto, Ontario: Ministry of Education.

Morrison, F., Bonyun, R., Pawley, C., & Walsh, M.
(1980). French proficiency and general progress:
Students in elementary core French programs,
1973-1980, and in immersion and bilingual programs, grades 8, 10 and 12 (7th annual report).
Ottawa, Ontario: Research Centre, Ottawa Board
of Education. (ERIC Document Reproduction Service No. ED 232 461)

Moskowitz, G. (1977). FLES methods courses now? ...
Yes, more than ever! Foreign Language Annals,
10, 277-80.

Muller, T.V. (1966). A comparison of two time
spacing arrangements in an elementary school
foreign language program (Doctoral dissertation,
University of California-Berkeley, 1966). Dissertation Abstracts International, 27/11A, 3781.
(Order No. 67-04977)

The National Commission on Excellence in Education.
(1983). A nation at risk: The imperative for
educational reform (Report No. 065-000-00177-2).
Washington, DC: U.S. Government Printing Office.
(ERIC Document Reproduction Service No. ED 226
006)

Newmark, G., Sweigert, R.L., Johnson, D.W., Mueller,
K.A., Melargno, R.J., & Silberman, H.F. (1966).
A field test of three approaches to the teaching
of Spanish in elementary schools. Sacramento,
CA: California State Department of Education.

(ERIC Document Reproduction Service No. ED 013 041)

New York (City) Board of Education. (1966). Italian in the elementary schools. Curriculum Bulletin, 1965-1966 (Series No. 9).

New York State Association of Foreign Language Teachers. (1972). Why FLES? A rationale for beginning foreign languages at the elementary school level. New York: Author. (Available from Robert J. Ludwig, 1102 Ardsley Road, Schenectady, N.Y. 12308)

Nolan, W.J. (1968). FLES and FLES teacher preparation in Kansas in 1967-1968 (Doctoral dissertation, University of Kansas, 1968). Dissertation Abstracts International, 30/02-A, 605. (Order No. 11237)

Oates, M.D. (1980). A non-intensive FLES program in French. French Review, 53, 507-13.

Oberding, B., & Onofrietto, M.H.M. (1982). Schlumpf-treffen II: Total immersion weekend New Jersey style. Foreign Language Annals, 15, 355-57.

O'Cherony, R. (1966). FLES status and teacher preparation. Hispania, 49, 121-25.

Offenberg, R.M., Montalvo, M., & Brown, E.K. (1971). Evaluation of the elementary school (FLES) Latin program 1970-71. Philadelphia, PA: School District of Philadelphia, Office of Research and Evaluation. (ERIC Document Reproduction Service No. ED 056 612)

*Oller, J. (Ed.). (1983). Issues in language testing research. Rowley, MA: Newbury House.

Oller, J.W., Jr., & Nagato, N. (1974). The long-term effect of FLES: An experiment. Modern Language Journal, 58(1-2), 15-19.

*Oller, J., & Perkins, K. (Eds.). (1980). Research in language testing. Rowley, MA: Newbury House.

O'Neil, C. (1974). Teaching of modern languages in primary schools. Educational Media International, 3, 26-29.

Oneto, A.J. (1968a). The effect on foreign language skill development of a continuing foreign language program beginning in the elementary grades (Doctoral dissertation, Kent State University,

1968). <u>Dissertation Abstracts International</u>,
29/12-A, 4193. (Order No. 69-09565)

*Oneto, A.J. (Comp). (1968b). <u>FLES evaluation: Lan-
guage skills and pupil attitudes in the Fairfield, Connecticut, Public Schools</u>. Hartford,
CT: Connecticut State Department of Education.
(ERIC Document Reproduction Service No. ED 023
333)

Ornstein, J. (1966). A frank appraisal: The foreign
language program in our grade schools. <u>The Education Digest</u>, <u>31</u>(8), 22-25.

Ornstein, J., & Lado, R. (1967). Research in foreign
language teaching methodology. <u>International
Review of Applied Linguistics</u>, <u>5</u>(1), 11-25.

Ornstein-Galicia, J.L., & Penfield, J. (1981). A
problem-solving model for integrating science and
language in bilingual/bicultural education.
<u>Bilingual Education Paper Series</u>, <u>5</u>(1). Los
Angeles: California State University, Evaluation, Dissemination and Assessment Center. (ERIC
Document Reproduction Service No. ED 164 128)

Otto, F.R. (1966). An assessment of three approaches
to staffing and implementing the elementary
foreign language program (Doctoral dissertation,
University of Wisconsin, 1966). <u>Dissertation
Abstracts International</u>, <u>28</u>/02A, 439. (Order No.
66-09951)

Otto, F.R. (1968). Alternative approaches to staffing the elementary foreign language program:
Cost and time vs. achievement and satisfaction.
<u>Modern Language Journal</u>, <u>52</u>, 293-301.

Otto, F.R. (1969). A survey of FLES teacher certification requirements. <u>Modern Language Journal</u>,
<u>53</u>, 93-94.

*Oyama, S. (1976). A sensitive period for the acqui-
sition of a non-native phonological system.
<u>Journal of Psycholinguistic Research</u>, <u>5</u>, 261-85.

Ozete, O. (1980). Milwaukee's French/German/Spanish
immersion success. <u>Hispania</u>, <u>63</u>, 569-71.

*Page, M.M. (1966). We dropped FLES. <u>Modern Lan-
guage Journal</u>, <u>50</u>, 139-41.

Parrott, G.A. (1967). Criteria for evaluating
foreign language program articulation between
elementary and secondary levels (Doctoral disser-

tation, University of Southern California, 1967).
Dissertation Abstracts International, 28/01-A,
58. (Order No. 67-08022)

Patterson, D.F. (1969). An historical, descriptive
study of the television teaching of Spanish in
the Detroit Public Schools following the principles of foreign languages in the elementary
school (FLES) (Doctoral dissertation, University
of Michigan, 1969). _Dissertation Abstracts In-
ternational_, 30/05-A, 2184. (Order No. 69-18077)

Patterson, E.G. (1965). FLES and beginning Latin.
The Classical Journal, 6(2), 60-62.

Pawley, C. (1983, April). _Ten years of immersion in
the Ottawa area_. Paper presented at the annual
meeting of the American Educational Research
Association, Montreal, Quebec. (ERIC Document
Reproduction Service No. ED 231 216)

Pesola, C. (In press). _A source book for elementary
and middle school language programs_ (rev. ed.).
Minneapolis: Minnesota State Department of
Education.

Pillet, R.A. (Ed.). (1967). _F.L.E.S and the objec-
tives of the contemporary elementary schools_
(Report by the FLES Committee of the American
Association of Teachers of French). Philadel-
phia, PA: Chilton. (ERIC Document Reproduction
Service No. ED 081 293)

Pillet, R.A. (1968). The impact of FLES: An appraisal. _Modern Language Journal_, 52, 486-90.

*Pillet, R.A. (1974). _Foreign language study: Per-
spective and prospect_. Chicago: The University
of Chicago Press.

Pimsleur, P. (1980). _How to learn a foreign language_
(The Foreign and Second Language Educator
Series). Boston: Heinle & Heinle.

*Plann, S. (1976). _The Spanish immersion program:
Towards native-like proficiency or a classroom
dialect?_ Unpublished master's thesis, University
of California-Los Angeles.

Plann, S. (1977). Acquiring a second language in an
immersion classroom. In D. Brown, C. Yorio, & R.
Crymes (Eds.), _On TESOL '77_, 213-25.

Plann, S. (1979). Morphological problems in the
acquisition of Spanish in an immersion classroom.

In R.W. Andersen (Ed.), <u>The acquisition and use</u>
<u>of Spanish and English as first and second lan-</u>
<u>guages</u>. Washington, DC: Teachers of English to
Speakers of Other Languages.

*Popham, J. (1975). <u>Educational evaluation</u>. Engle-
wood Cliffs, NJ: Prentice-Hall.

Potts, M.H. (1967). Effect of second-language
instruction on reading proficiency and general
school achievement of primary-grade children.
<u>American Educational Research Journal</u>, <u>4</u>(4),
367-73.

*Prator, C., & Celce-Murcia, M. (1979). An outline
of language teaching approaches. In M. Celce-
Murcia (Ed.), <u>Teaching English as a second or</u>
<u>foreign language</u>. Rowley, MA: Newbury House.

*President's Commission on Foreign Language and
International Studies. (1979). <u>Strength through</u>
<u>wisdom: A critique of U.S. capability</u> (Report to
the President). Washington, DC: U.S. Government
Printing Office. (ERIC Document Reproduction
Service No. ED 176 599)

Ratté, E.H. (1968). Foreign language and the elementary school language arts program. <u>The French</u>
<u>Review</u>, <u>42</u>, 80-85.

Rhodes, J.W. (1971). Can FLES bolster general education? <u>Die Unterrichtspraxis</u>, <u>4</u>(1), 133-34.

*Rhodes, N.C. (1981). Foreign language in the
elementary school: A status report. <u>ERIC/CLL</u>
<u>News Bulletin</u>, <u>5</u>(1), 1, 7.

*Rhodes, N.C. (1983). Are languages making a come-
back? <u>Principal</u>, <u>62</u>(4), 24-28.

*Rhodes, N.C., & Schreibstein, A.R. (1983). <u>Foreign</u>
<u>language in the elementary school: A practical</u>
<u>guide</u>. Washington, DC: Center for Applied Lin-
guistics. (ERIC Document Reproduction Service
No. ED 225 403)

*Rhodes, N.C., & Snow, M.A. (1984). Foreign language
in the elementary school: A comparison of
achievement. <u>ERIC/CLL News Bulletin</u>, <u>7</u>(2), 3-5.

*Rhodes, N.C., Tucker, G.R., & Clark, J.L.D. (1981).
<u>Elementary school foreign language instruction</u>
<u>in the United States: Innovative approaches for</u>
<u>the 1980s. Final Report</u>. Washington, DC:

Center for Applied Linguistics. (ERIC Document
Reproduction Service No. ED 209 940)

*Rickards, G.E. (1984). Parental attitude in the San
Diego area regarding foreign language study at
the elementary school level (Doctoral dissertation, United States International University,
1984). Dissertation Abstracts International,
45/05-A, 1262-A. (Order No. DA8417509) (ERIC
Document Reproduction Service No. ED 245 532)

*Rockford (IL) Public Schools. (1983). Learning a
second language--differentiating elementary
gifted curriculum. (Project proposal; available
from Muldoon Center, Rockford, IL 61100).

Rothfarb, S.H. (1970). Teacher-pupil interaction in
the FLES class. Hispania, 53, 256-60.

Ryan, H.M. (1961). The effects of foreign language
study in the elementary school (FLES) on first
year achievement in a second language (Doctoral
dissertation, Pennsylvania State University,
1961). Dissertation Abstracts International,
22/11, 3910. (Order No. 62-01737)

San Diego City Schools. (1980). ILP (Intercultural
Language Program) students again score above
expectancy in achievement. ILP Newsletter, 3(1),
1, 4.

Scherer, F.H. (1958). A descriptive survey of foreign language offerings in the public elementary
schools in the eight counties of western New York
state (Doctoral dissertation, State University of
New York at Buffalo, 1958). Dissertation Abstracts International, 19/12, 3178. (Order No.
59-01515)

*Schinke-Llano, L. (1984). Programmatic and instruc-
tional aspects of language immersion programs.
Unpublished manuscript. (Available from SRA
Technologies, 2570 W. El Camino Real, Ste. 402,
Mountain View, CA 94040)

Schrade, A.O. (1972). Children's responses toward
Spanish cultures through the integration of FLES,
language arts and social studies (Doctoral
dissertation, Ohio State University, 1972).
Dissertation Abstracts International, 33/11-A,
6224. (Order No. DDJ73-11571)

Schrade, A.O. (1978). Des Plaines FLES: Successful
    language arts and social studies integration.
    Hispania, 61, 504-07.
*Schumann, J. (1975). Affective factors and the
    problem of age in second language acquisition.
    Language Learning, 25, 209-35.
Shmarak, A., Dostal, N., Harris, C., del Barrio, M.M.,
    & McArthur, J. (1965). T.V. FLES matures in the
    Detroit Public Schools: A symposium on tele-
    vision teaching. Modern Language Journal, 49,
    207-19, 248.
*Scott, S. (1973). The relation of divergent think-
    ing to bilingualism: Cause or effect? Montreal,
    Quebec: McGill University. Unpublished.
Scully, M.G. (1977). An end to the decline in lan-
    guage study? The Chronicle of Higher Education,
    15(15), 1.
*Seliger, H.W., Krashen, S., & Ladefoged, P. (1975).
    Maturational constraints in the acquisition of
    native-like accent in second language learning.
    Language Science, 36, 20-22.
Shapson, S.M., & Day, E.M. (1983, March). Evaluation
    studies of bilingual programs in Canada. Paper
    presented at the annual meeting of the American
    Educational Research Association, Montreal,
    Quebec. (ERIC Document Reproduction Service No.
    ED 228 889)
Shelton, H. (1968, August). FLES, A pattern for
    growth. Paper presented at the national conven-
    tion of the American Association of Teachers of
    Spanish and Portuguese, San Antonio, TX. (ERIC
    Document Reproduction Service No. ED 030 340)
Simon, P. (1980). The tongue-tied American: Con-
    fronting the foreign language crisis. New York:
    Continuum.
Smith, W.H. (1966). Linguistic and academic achieve-
    ment of elementary students studying a foreign
    language (Doctoral dissertation, Colorado State
    University, 1966). Dissertation Abstracts Inter-
    national, 27/11-A, 3882. (Order No. 67-06086)
Smythe, P.C., Stennet, R.G., & Gardner, R.C. (1975).
    The best age for foreign-language training:
    Issues, options and facts. Canadian Modern Lan-
    guage Review, 32(1), 10-23.

BIBLIOGRAPHY   97

*Snow, C., & Hoefnagel-Höhle, M. (1977). Age differ-
    ences in the pronunciation of foreign sounds.
    Language and Speech, 20, 357-65.
Snow, M.A. (1977). The immersion technique of bilin-
    gual education: The St. Lambert and Culver City
    models. Unpublished manuscript, University of
    California-Los Angeles.
Snow, M.A. (1979). Self-report of attitudes and lan-
    guage use by students in a Spanish immersion
    program. Unpublished master's thesis, University
    of California-Los Angeles.
Snow, M.A. (1983). Graduates of the Culver City
    Spanish immersion program: A follow-up report.
    Unpublished paper, University of California-Los
    Angeles.
Snow, M.A., Galván, J.L., & Campbell, R.N. (1983).
    The pilot class of the Culver City Spanish immer-
    sion program: A follow-up report after the
    seventh grade or what ever happened to the immer-
    sion class of '78? In K. Bailey, M. Long, & S.
    Peck (Eds.), Second language acquisition studies.
    Rowley, MA: Newbury House.
Sparkman, L. (Ed.). (1966). Culture in the FLES
    program. Philadelphia: Chilton Book Co. (ERIC
    Document Reproduction Service No. ED 081 294)
*Spilka, I. (1976). Assessment of second-language
    performance in immersion programs. Canadian
    Modern Language Review, 32, 543-61.
Staff. (1981). Foreign language instruction in the
    elementary school: Advisory group convenes. The
    Linguistic Reporter, 23(7), 1-2, 6.
*Stern, H.H. (1963). Foreign languages in primary
    education, Conference on the Teaching of Foreign
    or Second Languages to Younger Children,
    (Hamburg, Apr. 9-14, 1962). New York: UNESCO.
    (ERIC Document Reproduction Service No. ED 013
    031)
Stern, H.H. (1973). Bilingual education: A review
    of recent North American experience. Modern
    Languages, 54, 57-62.
*Stern, H.H. (1976). Optimal age: Myth or reality?
    Canadian Modern Language Review, 32, 283-94.
Stern, H.H., Burstall, C., & Harley, B. (1975).
    French from age eight, or eleven? Toronto,

Ontario: Ontario Ministry of Education and
Ontario Institute for Studies in Education.
Stern, H.H., Swain, M., McLean, L.D., Friedman, R.G.,
Harley, B., & Lapkin, S. (1976). French programs: Some major issues. Evaluation and synthesis of studies related to the experimental
programs for the teaching of French as a second
language in the Carleton-Ottawa school boards.
Ottawa, Ontario: University of Ottawa Press.
Stern, H.H., Swain, M., & McLean, L.D. (1976).
Three approaches to teaching French: Evaluation
and overview of studies related to the federally-
funded extensions of the second language learning (French) programs in the Carleton and Ottawa
school boards. Ottawa, Ontario: University of
Ottawa Press.
Stevens, E. (1974). Techniques for FLES and other
levels. Hispania, 57, 79-83.
Stevens, F. (1982, May). Activity-centred approaches
to second language learning. Paper presented at
the 16th annual convention of Teachers of English
to Speakers of Other Languages, Honolulu, HI.
(ERIC Document Reproduction Service No. ED 221
066)
Strasheim, L. (1982). FLEX: The acronym and the
entity. Die Unterrichtspraxis, 15, 60-63.
Strauss, G. (1973). French for oral fluency for the
primary teacher trainee. Babel, 9(3), 7-9, 15.
*Swain, M. (1975). Writing skills of grade three
French immersion pupils. Working Papers on
Bilingualism, 7, 1-38.
Swain, M. (1978a). French immersion: Early, late or
partial? Canadian Modern Language Review, 34,
577-85.
Swain, M. (1978b). School reform through bilingual
education: Problems and some solutions in eva-
luating programs. Comparative Education Review,
22(3), 420-33.
*Swain, M. (1980). French immersion programs in
Canada. Multi-Culturalism, 4, 3-6.
Swain, M. (1981). Bilingual education for majority
and minority language children. Studia Linguis-
tica, 35(1-2), 15-32.
Swain, M. (1981b). Linguistic expectations: Core,

extended and immersion programs. The Canadian
Modern Language Review, 37, 486-97.

Swain, M. (1983, October). Communicative competence:
Some roles of comprehensible input and compre-
hensible output in its development. Paper pre-
sented at the 10th University of Michigan
Conference on Applied Linguistics, University of
Michigan, Ann Arbor.

*Swain, M. (1984a). A review of immersion education
in Canada: Research and evaluation studies. In
Studies on immersion education:A collection for
United States educators. Sacramento, CA:
California State Department of Education (ERIC
Document Reproduction Service No. ED 239 509)

Swain, M. (1984b). Teaching and testing communica-
tively. TESL Talk, 15(1-2), 7-18.

*Swain, M., & Lapkin, S. (1982). Evaluating bilin-
gual education: A Canadian case study.
Clevedon, UK: Multilingual Matters.

Swain, M., Lapkin, S., & Andrew, C.M. (1981). Early
French immersion later on. Journal of Multilingual and Multicultural Development, 2(1), 1-23.

*Taylor, B. (1974). Toward a theory of language
acquisition. Language Learning, 24, 23-35.

*Terrell, T.D. (1977). A natural approach to second
language acquisition and learning. Modern Language Journal, 61, 325-37.

Thimmesch, N. (1981, February). Our shocking
illiteracy in foreign languages. Reader's
Digest, pp. 175-80.

Thompson, R.A., & Blackwell, J.M. (1974). FLES: To
be or not to be. Elementary English, 51, 541-43,
556.

Trites, R.L., & Price, M.A. (1980). Assessment of
readiness for primary French immersion: Grade
one follow-up assessment. Ottawa, Ontario:
University of Ottawa Press. (ERIC Document
Reproduction Service No. ED 218 980)

Trujillo, L.A., Quiat, M., & Valenzuela, X. (1982).
Foreign language camps: Jefferson County Public
Schools R-1. Lakewood, CO: Jefferson County
Public Schools. (ERIC Document Reproduction
Service No. ED 226 582)

*Tucker, G.R. (1980). Implications for U.S. bilingual education: Evidence from Canadian research. Focus, 2, 1-2.

Tucker, G.R. (1983). The role of language in education: Evidence from North America and the developing world. In R.J. Di Pietro, W. Frawley, & A. Wedel (Eds.), The first Delaware symposium on language studies--Selected papers (pp. 35-44). East Brunswick, NJ: Associated University Presses.

Tucker, G.R., Hamayan, E., & Genesee, F. (1976). Affective, cognitive and social factors in second-language acquisition. Canadian Modern Language Review, 32, 214-26.

Turner, L.O. (1962). A study of foreign language instruction in the public elementary schools of Virginia, 1959-1960 (Doctoral dissertation, University of Virginia, 1962). Dissertation Abstracts International, 23/11, 4176. (Order No. 63-01961)

20th Century Fund Task Force in Federal Elementary and Secondary Education Policy. (1983). Making the grade (Report of task force and background paper by Paul E. Peterson). New York: Author. (ERIC Document Reproduction Service No. ED 233 112)

*Urbanski, H. (1982). Summer and weekend language immersion programs at New Paltz. ADFL Bulletin, 13(4), 10-11.

*Valette, R.M. (1977). Modern language testing: A handbook (2nd ed.). New York: Harcourt, Brace, Jovanovich.

*Vines, L. (1983). A guide to language camps in the U.S.: 2. Washington, DC: ERIC Clearinghouse on Languages and Linguistics. (ERIC Document Reproduction Service No. ED 226 603)

Vocolo, J.M. (1967). The effect of foreign language study in the elementary school upon achievement in the same foreign language in the high school. Modern Language Journal, 51, 463-69.

Von Wittich, B. (1971). The impact of method of evaluation upon achievement in elementary foreign language courses (Doctoral dissertation, Iowa State University, 1971). Dissertation Abstracts International, 32/10-A, 5576. (Order No. 72-12610)

*Walberg, H. (1974). Evaluating educational performance: A sourcebook of methods, instruments and examples. Berkeley, CA: McCutchan Publishing.

Waldman, E. (1975). Cross-ethnic attitudes of Anglo students in Spanish immersion, bilingual, and English schooling. Unpublished master's thesis, University of California at Los Angeles.

*Walker, R.L. (1984). Our schools are fortifying foreign language study. American School Board Journal, 171(6), 32.

Wallace, J.L. (1977). A program for teaching French in grades 3-5. Foreign Language Annals, 10, 271-75.

Wantagh Public Schools. (1968). Evaluation of foreign language in the elementary school. Wantagh, NY: Author. (ERIC Document Reproduction Service No. ED 025 975)

Weissman, J. (1978). Strategies of communication in the Culver City Spanish immersion program. Unpublished master's thesis, University of California-Los Angeles.

Wellborn, S.N. (1981, April 27). The bilingual American: Endangered species. U.S. News & World Report, pp. 57-58.

Wheeler, W.J. (1960). A survey of opinion of parents and teachers in Waukegan City School District Number 61 Waukegan, Illinois, on foreign language instruction in elementary schools (Doctoral dissertation, Northwestern University, 1960). Dissertation Abstracts International, 21/11, 3383. (Order No. 60-04813)

Wheetley, D.W. (1965). T.V. teaching of foreign languages results of a three year study. Ill. Ed., vol?(no.?), 246.

Wickstrom, D.R. (1964). Administrative policies and practices of elementary school foreign language programs in the Unified School Districts of California (Doctoral dissertation, University of Southern California, 1964). Dissertation Abstracts International, 25/06, 3373. (Order No. 64-12526)

Willford, M.L. (1979). The answer: High school foreign languages tutoring program. Foreign Language Annals, 12, 213-14.

*Wilson, S. (1977). The use of ethnographic techniques in educational research. Review of Educational Research, 47(2), 245-65.

Wood, L.T. (1972). A study of student attitudes towards foreign languages in public secondary schools of Utah. Unpublished master's thesis, Brigham Young University. (ERIC Document Reproduction Service No. ED 073 711)

Yamada, J., Takatsuka, S., Kotake, N., & Kurusu, J. (1980). On the optimum age for teaching foreign vocabulary to children. International Review of Applied Linguistics in Language Teaching, 18, 245-47.

Young, E.S. (1973). The modification of a middle school curriculum using the perceptions of early adolescents (Doctoral dissertation, Columbia University, 1973). Dissertation Abstracts International, 34/05A, 2285. (Order No. DDJ73-25174)

CURRICULUM GUIDES AND PROGRAM EVALUATIONS FROM
PUBLIC SCHOOL SYSTEMS AND UNIVERSITIES

Note: *Asterisks indicate works that are cited in the*
text.

ANNE ARUNDEL COUNTY (MD.) PUBLIC SCHOOLS

Foreign Language Experience in the Elementary School:
    French. 1980. Program guides include objectives,
    teaching guidelines for classroom teachers and
    volunteers, and a 9-unit curriculum. (ERIC Docu-
    ment Reproduction Service No. ED 218 984; German,
    ED 218 982; Spanish, ED 218 983)

BRITISH COLUMBIA DEPARTMENT OF EDUCATION,
CURRICULUM DEVELOPMENT BRANCH, VICTORIA

Elementary French Program Guide. 1976. Contains a
    rationale for offering French at the elementary
    level and an indication of the skills and apti-
    tudes pupils might acquire. (ERIC Document Repro-
    duction Service No. ED 176 550)
Elementary French Resource Book. 1976. Provides teach-
    ers with invaluable assistance in selecting
    appropriate FLES resources--books, tapes, kits,
    films, and commercial programs--and includes
    extensive evaluations of each. (ERIC Document
    Reproduction Service No. ED 176 551)
Practical Handbook for Learning Assistance Teachers in
    Early French Immersion (Manuel Pratique pour les
    Orthopédagogues: Immersion Précoce). 1981. Pro-
    vides guidelines for teachers who assist early
    French immersion students with learning problems
    such as problems with psychomotor functions, per-
    ception, visual and auditory memory, language
    development, and mathematics. (ERIC Document
    Reproduction Service No. ED 232 451)
Transitional English Language Arts Resource Manual:
    Grade 3. Early Immersion (Manuel de Ressources
    Programme de Transition Anglais-3e Année. Immer-

sion Précoce). 1981. Provides guidelines to
assist teachers of grade 3 French immersion
pupils in developng a concentrated English
language arts program to enable them to attain
competency in the essential basic skills. (ERIC
Document Reproduction Service No. ED 232 452)

BRITISH COLUMBIA DEPARTMENT OF EDUCATION, DIVISION OF
PUBLIC INSTRUCTION, VICTORIA

Early French Immersion: Kindergarten French (Immersion
Française Précoce: Français-Maternelle). 1981.
This teaching manual is based on general and
specific learning objectives for developing
listening, speaking, reading, and writing skills.
(ERIC Document Reproduction Service No. ED 231
230)
Early French Immersion: Kindergarten (Immersion
Française Précoce: Français-Maternelle). 1981.
Resource manual and teaching guide for the
kindergarten teacher in the early French immersion program that provides theoretical background
information, exercises, ways of presenting
material, resource materials, and lesson content.
(ERIC Document Reproduction Service No. ED 231
231)
Early French Immersion: French 1 (Immersion Française
Précoce: Français 1). 1981. Manual for first-
grade French immersion instruction, based on
general and specific learning objectives in
developing listening, speaking, reading, and
writing skills. (ERIC Document Reproduction Service No. ED 231 232; French 2, ED 231 233; French
3, ED 231 234; French 4, ED 231 235; French 5, ED
231 236; French 6, ED 231 237; French 7, ED 231
238)
Early French Immersion: Mathematics 1-7 (Immersion
Française Précoce: Mathématique 1-7). 1981.
Curriculum guide for French immersion instruction
in mathematics for grades 1-7 that lists text-
books and gives theoretical overview, application
notes, objectives, activities, and resource
lists. (ERIC Document Reproduction Service No.

ED 231 239; Social Studies, ED 213 240; Natural
Sciences, ED 231 241; Music, ED 231 242; Physical
Education, ED 231 243; Plastic Arts, ED 231 244)
Early French Immersion: Administrator's Resource Book
(Immersion Française Précoce). 1981. Handbook (in
English) to series of program teaching guides
(all in French) that serves as guide for adminis-
trators of near-total French immersion programs
for grades 1-7, covering staffing, scheduling,
enrollment, and program administration. (ERIC
Document Reproduction Service No. ED 231 246)
Early French Immersion: Teacher's Resource Book
(Immersion Française Précoce). 1981. Resource
book (in English) designed for teachers who are
new to early French immersion program for grades
1-7, giving suggestions, practical information,
examples of methodology, and references. (ERIC
Document Reproduction Service No. ED 231 245)

BRITISH COLUMBIA TEACHER'S FEDERATION, VANCOUVER

A Handbook for Bilingual School Resource Centers (2nd
ed.). 1983. Provides guidelines for teacher-
librarians organizing bilingual school resource
centers at British Columbia schools with French
immersion programs, providing handling, selection, acquisition, budgeting, terminology. (ERIC
Document Reproduction Service No. ED 232 450)

CENTRE FOR INFORMATION ON LANGUAGE TEACHING
AND RESEARCH, LONDON, U.K.

Teaching Materials for French. 1980. By E.W. Brown
(Comp.). Describes materials designed for use in
all areas of French language teaching and
obtainable in the United Kingdom. (ERIC Document
Reproduction Service No. ED 208 669.

CHICAGO (ILL.) BOARD OF EDUCATION

Sounds of Language. 1980. Describes a course that provides students with a greater understanding of
how language works and introduces them to the
variations of sound and structure of many languages. (ERIC Document Reproduction Service No.
ED 221 022)

CINCINNATI (OH.) PUBLIC SCHOOLS

Bilingual Programs: Curriculum French-Spanish (vol.
1). 1975. Volume of bilingual programs that
enunciates basic framework of program dealing
with the rationale, philosophy, and general goals
and objectives. (ERIC Document Reproduction Service No. ED 204 999)
* French Bilingual Program: Level III. 1978a.
(FL 011 633).
* Spanish Bilingual Program Curriculum Guide (Elementary Schools): Level I (2nd rev.). 1978b. By
M. Met. Provides content of the curriculum, performance objectives of each unit, and suggested
means for achieving desired outcomes for Level I.
(ERIC Document Reproduction Service No. ED 205
000)
* Spanish Bilingual Program: Level II (2nd rev.)
1978c. By M. Met. Provides content of the cur-
riculum, performance objectives of each unit, and
suggested means for achieving desired outcomes
for Level II. (ERIC Document Reproduction Service
No. ED 205 001).
Spanish Bilingual Program: Samples from Levels III and
IV. 1979. Presents sample lesson plans for Level
III and a more detailed sampling of Level IV.
(ERIC Document Reproduction Service No. ED 205
002)

DADE COUNTY (FLA.) FLES PROGRAM

Let's Speak Spanish Series. 1978 (2nd ed.). Audiolin-
gual materials with tapes. New York: McGraw-Hill
Book Co.

FAIRFAX (VA.) COUNTY PUBLIC SCHOOLS,
DIVISION OF ADULT SERVICES

* Elementary Foreign Language Teacher-PTA Liaison
  Handbook. 1978. Presents guidelines for teachers
  and PTA liaisons involved in the organization and
  implementation of an elementary school foreign
  language program. Provides supplemental elementary-level instruction for children in Spanish,
  French, German, Italian, Chinese, and Arabic.
  (ERIC Document Reproduction Service No. ED 223
  073)

FAIRFAX (VA.) COUNTY PUBLIC SCHOOLS, DEPARTMENT OF
VOCATIONAL, ADULT, AND COMMUNITY EDUCATION

* Elementary Foreign Language Guide to Resources.
  1982. Presents a program of studies, instructional resources, and suggestions for activities
  and materials for use by teachers in an elementary school foreign language program. (ERIC
  Document Reproduction Service No. ED 223 072)

FAIRMONT (W. VA.) STATE COLLEGE

Guide to French Videocassette Program for Elementary
  Schools, Grades 1-6. 1980. By L.E. Eckles & C.B.
  Sweeney. Provides scripts and accompanying activities for 18 videocassette French instruction
  programs for grades 1-6. (ERIC Document Reproduction Service No. ED 223 066)

INDIANA DEPARTMENT OF PUBLIC INSTRUCTION,
DIVISION OF CURRICULUM

* Introduction to French: Numbers, Colors, and Body/
  Clothing. 1981. Course and materials for use by
  classroom teachers in primary grades who may have
  no background in foreign language, intended as
  experiential or enrichment component of curriculum. (ERIC Document Reproduction No. ED 207 342;
  German, ED 207 344; Spanish, ED 207 343)

MILWAUKEE (WISC.) PUBLIC SCHOOLS

German Immersion Program: Second Grade Language Arts
   Curriculum. 1981. By T. Tarjan, J. Misslich, & R.
   Miller. Set of materials for use in the grade 2
   language arts curriculum, including worksheets
   and exercises for developing German vocabulary
   and grammar. (ERIC Document Reproduction Service
   No. ED 224 289)

A German Language Continuum: Kindergarten Through
   Grade 5. 1978. By G.E. Meyer. Rationale setting
   forth general and specific program goals and
   crieteria for evaluating communicative competence. Includes lists of sample exercises,
   topics. (ERIC Document Reproduction Service No.
   ED 191 257)

Helping Parents Learn a Second Language with Their
   Children: French. 1980. Compiled by A. Gradisnik.
   Guide for parents of elementary school children
   French language students who wish to learn French
   alongside their children. (ERIC Document Reproduction Service No. ED 208 653; German, ED 208
   654)

Multi-Language School: A Teacher's Guide. 1978. By
   A. Gradisnik & H. Anderson. Brief general
   description and rational of program, comparison
   with other immersion programs, classroom procedures, routines for lower, middle, and upper primary grades. (ERIC Document Reproduction Service
   No. ED 191 256)

* A Resource Kit of Foreign Language Immersion Materi-
   als from the Milwaukee Public Schools. 1982.
   Instructional materials for immersion program in
   French and German, dealing with class activities,
   school activities outside classroom, program
   management. (ERIC Document Reproduction Service
   No. ED 191 279; French, 224 288; German, 224 287;
   Second Grade Language Arts, 244 289)

PROTESTANT SCHOOL BOARD OF GREATER MONTREAL

A Comparison of Early Immersion and Classes d'Acceuil
   Programs at the Kindergarten Level. 1979.

Assesses the French language proficiency of students enrolled in two different programs at the kindergarten level: an early immersion program and a "classe d'acceuil" program. (ERIC Document Reproduction Service No. ED 225 372)

Some Observations on the Nature of Language Transfer in the Simultaneous Acquisition of Two Second Languages. 1981. By E. Adiv. Examines the occurrence of transfer in the simultaneous acquisition of French and Hebrew by 57 native English-speaking children in a primary grades French-Hebrew immersion program in Montreal. (ERIC Document Reproduction Service No. ED 225 370)

Starting French in Kindergarten: The Effects of Program, Mother Tongue and Other Linguistic Experience on Second Language Development. 1980. By E. Adiv. Assesses the French language proficiency of kindergarten students enrolled in a French early immersion program and two "classes d'acceuil"--a special program for non-French-speaking immigrant children. (ERIC Document Reproduction Service No. ED 225 368)

Does a Late Immersion Program Make a Difference to the Graduates? Research Report 82-09. By R. Bonyun. Surveys attitudes toward French language programs and future language plans among a sample of students who had participated in Ottawa school district bilingual programs. (ERIC Document Reproduction Service No. ED 233 595)

ONTARIO INSTITUTE FOR STUDIES IN EDUCATION

La Fête de La Ste-Catherine: Guide. 1981. By R. Ullmann & J. Scane. Presents a teacher's French-English guide to a cultural module that provides introductory reading materials for elementary-school French students. (ERIC Document Reproduction Service No. ED 209 915)

French Diagnostic Reading Tests for Early French Immersion Primary Classes, Grades 1, 2, & 3: Guide (Tests Diagnostiques de Lecture pour les Classes d'Immersion au Primaire, Prémière,

Deuxième et Troisième Années). 1982. By M.
Tourond. A French-English guide to French
diagnostic reading tests for French immersion
classes, grades one through three, is presented.
(ERIC Document Reproduction Service No. ED 224
278)
French Immersion: The Trial Balloon That Flew. 1983.
Addresses concerns of 11-15-year-old students in
French immersion program and their parents: their
level of achievement in French, English, and
other subjects, and potential for maintaining
French after leaving program. (ERIC Document
Reproduction Service No. ED 225 404)
Le Hockey (Hockey). Teacher's Guide. 1979. By
M. Balchunas & R. Ullmann. Includes teacher's
guide and tape transcript for module aimed at
elementary or secondary school students with goal
of teaching basic hockey vocabulary and understanding hockey games broadcast with French com-
mentary. (ERIC Document Reproduction Service No.
ED 180 255)
Le Mateo (The Weather Report). Teacher's Guide. 1973.
By R. Elsass et al. Includes resource kit for
teaching French at the intermediate level with
the aim of introducing elementary or secondary
school students to terminology used in French
radio broadcasts, and especially in weather
reports. (ERIC Document Reproduction Service No.
ED 180 257)
Les Papillons (The Butterflies). Teacher's Guide.
1972. By R. Elsass & J. Howard. Includes resource
kit for teaching French at the beginning primary
level; module centers around a children's story,
divided into 41 short episodes. (ERIC Document
Reproduction Service No. ED 180 258)
A Survey of French Immersion Materials (K-6). 1977.
Annotated list of material used at each grade
level for French immersion programs. (Available
from OISE, 252 Bloor St. West, Toronto M5S 1V6
Canada)
Le Temps des Sucres (Sugaring-Off Time). 1978. By
R. Ullmann, et al. Resource kit for teaching
French listening comprehension at the beginning
elementary level--includes teacher's guide with

sample activities and lesson plans and handbook
entitled "The Maple Sugar Industry." (ERIC Document Reproduction Service No. ED 180 248)

ORANGE COUNTY (FLA.)

Un Poquito de Espanol. A "Point of Departure" Outline
for Volunteer Spanish Teachers in the Elementary
School. 1977. Manual used by volunteer teachers
to teach conversational Spanish. (ERIC Document
Reproduction Service No. ED 228 832)

OTTAWA BOARD OF EDUCATION

French Proficiency and General Progress: Students in
Elementary Core French Programs, 1973-1980, and
in Immersion and Bilingual Programs, Grades 8,
10, and 12, 1980. Evaluation of the Second
Language Learning (French) Programs in the
Schools of the Ottawa and Carleton Boards of Education Seventh Annual Report, December 1980.
1980. By F. Morrison, R. Bonyun, C. Pawley, & M.
Walsh. Reviews the effectiveness of alternative
programs for teaching French as a second language
in Ottawa and Carleton schools. (ERIC Document
Reproduction Service No. ED 232 461)

SAN DIEGO CITY SCHOOLS

Mathematics: Level A (Matematicas: Nivel A). 1980.
Teacher's manual for an elementary-level mathematics course in Spanish, part of an immersion
program for English-speaking children. Manual for
kindergarten and first-grade pupils. (ERIC Document Reproduction Service No. ED 232 455; Spanish
Mathematics Level E, ED 232 456; Spanish Mathematics Level F, ED 232 457; Spanish Science Level
A, ED 232 459; French Mathematics Level A, ED 232
458)
Spanish Language Arts for the English Speaker. 1980.
By J. Wraith (Chairperson, Intercultural Language

Program and Bilingual Education Program).
Teacher's guide and student and teacher workbooks
for the first level of a multilevel Spanish language arts program. (ERIC Document Reproduction
Service No. ED 232 460; Level B, ED 234 646)

WINTHROP COLLEGE (ROCK HILL, S.C.)

A FLES Handbook: French, Spanish, German, Grades K-6
(3rd ed., rev.). 1979. By Dorothy Medlin. Gives
classroom activities, lesson planning for FLES.
(ERIC Document Reproduction Service No. ED 209
942)

OTHER PUBLICATIONS

MCGRAW-HILL BOOK COMPANY, WEBSTER DIVISION

A Cada Paso: Lengua, Lectura, y Cultura. 1978. By C.J.
Schmidt. Elementary school texts designed for
Spanish speakers in bilingual programs (levels
1-4) that provide Spanish language development
and basic social studies concepts.

MCMILLAN PUBLISHING CO., NEW YORK

Hola, Amigos! 1979. Elementary to junior high-level,
well-illustrated materials for a Spanish FLES
program.

NATIONAL TEXTBOOK CO., SKOKIE, ILL.

Asi Escribimos, Ya Escribimos, A Escribir! 1977. By
Alice Mohrman. Three-workbook series containing
writing exercises to help pupils reinforce and
develop knowledge of Spanish language structure.
Let's Play Games in Spanish, Book 1. 1980. Gives conversational and vocabulary-building activities to
help teach basic Spanish conversation to grades
K-8.

Lotería, Creative Vocabulary/Verb Bingo Games for Student Mastery and Review. 1979. Set of 32 games aid in building and reinforcing vocabulary; set of 32 duplicating masters includes games to review tenses singly and in combination.

TEXAS EDUCATION AGENCY, AUSTIN DIV. OF CURRICULUM DEVELOPMENT

Spanish K-Grade 2: A Guide for Teachers. 1981. Guide that identifies objectives for the teaching of Spanish in K-2 and provides ideas for developing language and culture skills in children. (ERIC Document Reproduction Service No. ED 203 666)

IMMERSION AND PARTIAL IMMERSION LANGUAGE PROGRAMS

School System	Comments	Number of Pupils and Grades
Alpine (UT) School District	Started in 1978; local funding; total immersion.	123 1-6
Baton Rouge (LA)	Started in 1978; local funding; total immersion.	60 K-4
Cincinnati (OH) Public Schools	Started in 1974; local funding; magnet schools articulated with junior and senior high; total immersion (2 Spanish, 2 French); partial immersion in 4 schools; curriculum integrated in 5 schools (1 French, 1 German, 3 Spanish); 1 middle school.	Total immersion 500 Spanish 600 French Curriculum-integrated 300 French 450 German 550 Spanish 400 Middle
Culver City (CA)	Started in 1971; local funding; total immersion; magnet school.	120
Davis (CA)	Started in 1982, total immersion; local funding and parental assistance in 2 schools.	89 K-3
Detroit (MI)	Started in 1981; tuition; corporate funding; government of France; total immersion; independent school; begins with bilingual preschool; 55% native French speakers.	135
Detroit (MI)	Started in 1984, kindergarten; plan to add a grade a year; local funding; total immersion; 4 days a week (no school Wednesday).	22

IN U.S. ELEMENTARY SCHOOLS, 1985

Numbers and/or Descriptions of Teachers	Languages	Contacts
5	Spanish	Janet Spencer, Principal Cherry Hill Elem. School 250 E. 1650 South Orem, UT 84057 (801) 225-3387
5	Spanish French	Mrs. Ben Peabody, Sr., Principal La Belle Aire Elementary School 12255 Tams Dr. Baton Rouge, LA 70815 (504) 275-7480
29 Total immersion 68 Curriculum-integrated	French German Spanish	Nelida Mietta-Fontana, Supervisor Cincinnati Public Schools 230 E. 9th St. Cincinnati, OH 45202 (513) 369-4937
4	Spanish	Eugene Ziff, Principal El Rincon Elem. School 11177 Overland Ave. Culver City, CA 90230 (213) 839-5285
3	Spanish	Floyd Fenocchio Davis Joint Unified Schools Dist. 526 B. St. Davis, CA 95616 (916) 756-0144
15 full-time 5 part-time	French	Jean François Genay, Director Lycee International School 30800 Evergreen School Southfield, MI 48076 (313) 642-1178
1	Spanish	Lydia Engel, Teacher Fairbanks Elem. School 8000 John C. Lodge St. Detroit, MI 48202 (313) 494-2317

School System	Comments	Number of Pupils and Grades
Eugene (OR) District 4J	Started in 1983; local funding; partial immersion in 2 magnet schools; program began with primary grades and will continue to expand through middle school and culminate in the development of an international high school program.	150 50
Ft. Worth (TX)	Started in 1983; partial immersion in 3 schools; local funding.	166 K-3
Holliston (MA)	Started in 1979; local funding; French total immersion K-4, partial immersion 5-8; Spanish partial immersion offered in middle school.	125
Long Beach (CA)	Started in 1975; at first, Title VII funding, currently local funding; partial immersion: basics in first language, 1 hour in second language instruction; all other courses in second language.	360 6 Spanish classes 6 English classes
Milwaukee (WI) Public Schools	Started in 1977; local funding; total immersion in 3 elementary schools: begins with 4-yr.-old kindergarten; curriculum-integrated middle school: social studies and language arts class in second language.	German K-8 290 French K-7 280 Spanish K-5 270 Middle school, 45

Numbers and/or Descriptions of Teachers	Languages	Contacts
7.5	Spanish	Ernie Carabajal, Principal Meadowlark Bilingual School 1500 Queens Way Eugene, OR 97401 (503) 687-3368
2.5	French	Sally Walker, Principal Harris French School 1150 E. 29th Ave. Eugene, OR 97405 (503) 687-3286
8	Spanish	Annette Lowry Foreign Language Dept. Ft. Worth Ind. School District 3210 W. Lancaster Ft. Worth, TX 76107 (817) 336-8311 (Ext. 630)
5	French	James Palladino, Principal Miller Elementary School Woodland St. Holliston, MA 01746 (617) 429-1601
12 6 native Spanish 6 native English	Spanish English	Betty Clement, Principal Patrick Henry Elementary School 3720 Canehill Ave. Long Beach, CA 90808 (213) 421-3754
26	German French Spanish	Helena Anderson-Curtain Foreign Language Curr. Specialist Milwaukee Public Schools P.O. Drawer 10K Milwaukee, WI 53201 (414) 475-8305

IMMERSION AND PARTIAL IMMERSION LANGUAGE PROGRAMS

School System	Comments	Number of Pupils and Grades
Montgomery County (MD) Public Schools	Started in 1978; local funding; Spanish total immersion; magnet school.	74
Montgomery County (MD) Public Schools	French total immersion started in 1974 at Four Corners Elementary School and now continuing at Oak View; Spanish partial immersion started 1984; small outside funding; articulation with junior high: one subject course per year for former immersion pupils.	238 Fr. 46 Sp.
Rochester (NY)	Started in 1981; local funding with additional Chapter II funds; total immersion (except for English reading) in 3 schools.	60 1-3
San Diego (CA)	Started in 1975; ESEA Title VII funding; bilingual immersion program (60% Spanish speakers, limited English proficient, 40% English speakers) in 6 schools.	550 preschool, K-6
San Diego (CA) City Schools	Started in 1977; special funding in initial years; regular funding now; total immersion for those who begin in K-2, partial for those who begin 3-6; partial immersion 7-12 in 6 schools including 2 secondary schools; magnet schools.	705 total imm. 95 partial imm.

Numbers and/or Descriptions of Participants	Languages	Contacts
3	Spanish	Louise Rosenberg, Principal Rock Creek Forest Elem. School 8330 Grubb Rd. Chevy Chase, MD 20815 (301) 589-0005
9 French 2 Spanish	French Spanish	Elizabeth Morgan, Principal Oak View Elementary School 400 E. Wayne Ave. Silver Spring, MD 20901 (301) 589-0020
3	Spanish	Alessio Evangelista Director, Foreign Lang. Dept. City School District 131 W. Broad St. Rochester, NY 14608 (716) 325-4560 (Ext. 2315)
19 Bilingual (Spanish/ English) 11 English	Spanish English	Eunice L. Lear, Project Director Bandini Center, B-1 3550 Logan Ave. San Diego, CA 92113 (619) 239-9101
43	French Spanish	Tim Allen, Curriculum Specialist Second Language Education San Diego Schools Educational Center 4100 Normal St. San Diego, CA 92103 (619) 293-8095

IMMERSION AND PARTIAL IMMERSION LANGUAGE PROGRAMS

School System	Comments	Number of Pupils and Grades
San Francisco (CA)	Started Spanish in 1983; started Chinese in 1984; local funding; total immersion in 2 schools; Spanish K-1: 90% immersion (English is oral enrichment; grade 2: 80% immersion (transfer to English reading); Chinese: 80% Chinese, 20% English (due to disparities between English and Chinese oral systems).	104
Tulsa (OK) Public Schools (Independent School District #1)	Started in 1981; local and federal funding; total immersion.	87
Washington (DC)	Started in 1966; tuition (independent school); partial immersion; nursery through grade 12; pupils represent 89 nationalities; staff represent 30 nationalities; international baccalaureate.	550
Washington (DC)	Started in 1971; local funding; partial immersion (50% English, 50% Spanish).	330 Pre K-6

Numbers and/or Descriptions of Teachers	Languages	Contacts
4	Spanish Cantonese	Lois Meyer Immersion Education Programs Bilingual Ed. Dept., SFUSD 300 Seneca Ave., Rm. 2 San Francisco, CA 94112 (415) 239-0518
4	Spanish	Roger Tomlinson, Principal Eliot Elementary School 1442 E. 36th St. Tulsa, OK 74105 (918) 743-9709
60 full-time equivalents	French Spanish	Dorothy Bruchholz Goodman, Director Washington International School 3100 Macomb St. NW Washington, DC 20008 (202) 364-1818
12 Spanish 12 English (1 resource Spanish; 1 resource English; 1 resource bilingual, math)	Spanish	Paquita Holland, Principal Oyster Elementary School 29th and Calvert Sts., NW Washington, DC 20008 (202) 673-7277

School System	Program Sponsorship	Comments	Number of Pupils and Grades
Baton Rouge (LA)	Louisiana Department of Education, Council for Development of French in Louisiana (CODOFIL), and Cordell Hull Foundation for International Education (New Orleans)	Started in 1971; daily classes during school day for 30 minutes in 33 parishes; state funding; governments of France, Belgium, Quebec, Mexico, and Hungary supply teachers and materials; state Board of Education has mandated foreign language study in grades 4-8 beginning in 1985, one grade per year.	K-6
Fairfax County (VA) Public Schools	County Department of Adult and Community Education, parents pay tuition covering salaries and materials	Started 1975; classes before and after school in 85 schools; 2 times/week for 45 minutes or once a week for an hour; parents pay tuition covering salaries and materials; emphasis on oral communication and cultural appreciation.	3,500 1-6
Lexington (MA)	School system (local funding)	Started 1957; 3 to 4 times a week for 30 minutes in 6 schools; emphasis on oral communication and cultural appreciation.	4-6

EXAMPLES OF PROGRAMS

THE ELEMENTARY SCHOOL (FLES) PROGRAMS, 1985

Numbers and/or Descriptions of Teachers	Languages	Contacts
Itinerant language teachers: 112 from foreign countries; 150 Louisiana State certified teachers	French Spanish Hungarian	Homer Dyess Bureau of Academic Support Foreign Langages and Bilingual Education Section State Department of Education P.O. Box 94064 Baton Rouge, LA 70804 (504) 342-3453
225; many native speakers; teacher certification not required	Spanish French German Latin American Sign	Susan Klein Coordinator of Community Education Pimmit Hills Center 7510 Lisle Ave. Falls Church, VA 22043 (703) 893-1090 (Ext. 11, 12)
6 part-time; have degrees in French or are native speakers	French	Anthony Bent Coordinator of Foreign Languages Lexington Public Schools 251 Waltham Street Lexington, MA 02173 (617) 862-7500

EXAMPLES OF PROGRAMS

School System	Program Sponsorship	Comments	Number of Pupils and Grades
Seattle (WA)	Seattle Language School (tuition)	Started in 1979; classes before or after school in 17 schools in 6 school districts in greater Seattle; 2 times/week for 45 minutes; emphasis on oral communication, listening comprehension, and cultural appreciation; private language school administers program at local public and private schools.	1-6
St. Louis (MO) Public Schools	School system (city-wide magnet schools) (local funding)	Started in 1976; daily classes during school day; emphasis on oral communication, pronunciation, basic vocabulary, and cultural appreciation.	240 K-8

CURRICULUM-INTEGRATED

| Chicago (IL) | Public schools (local funding) | Started in 1978; 6 desegregation magnet schools; curriculum-integrated. | 2,676 |

Numbers and/or Descriptions of Teachers	Languages	Contacts
24 part-time Teacher requirements: foreign language fluency; enthusiasm; willingness to travel to teach just for 45 minutes; ability to work with children	Spanish French German (other languages on request)	Ulrike Criminale The Language School YMCA Building 909 Fourth Avenue Seattle, WA 98104 (206) 682-6985
3	Spanish French German	Susan Walker Wilkinson School FLES 7212 Arsenal Street St. Louis, MO 63143 (314) 645-1202

APPROACH TO FLES

32	French German Italian Spanish Japanese Modern Greek Russian Polish	Edwin Cudecki, Director Bureau of Foreign Languages Chicago Public Schools 1819 W. Pershing Rd. 6 Center (C) Chicago, IL 60609 312-890-7995

School System	Program Sponsorship	Comments	Number of Pupils and Grades
Anne Arundel County (MD) Public Schools	School system (local funding)	Started in 1978; classes during and after school; once/week, 30-40 minutes; 54 of 70 schools in county have a volunteer program of FLEX; use curriculum material developed by county; basic introduction to foreign words, phrases, and conversation as well as aspects of the cultures.	4,317 2-6
Orange County (FL)	ADDitions School Volunteer Program (state money for volunteers and local funding)	Started in 1977; classes during school; 20-40 minutes daily, depending on grade; 33 of 67 schools requested program (112 classes); use teaching manual developed by county volunteer program; basic introduction to Spanish conversation with songs, games, and puppets.	K-6
State of Indiana	Indiana Dept. of Education under a grant from NEH, and local schools	Started in 1980; scheduling of instruction is a local option; materials have been disseminated to approx. 400 classroom teachers throughout state; use materials developed by State Department of Public Instruction (now called Dept. of Education); basic introduction to foreign sounds, words, phrases, and conversation as well as aspects of the culture through 4 units in each language: Introduction, Body/Clothing, Numbers, Colors; all 3 languages may be introduced to a class in one year	K-3

EXAMPLES OF PROGRAMS

(FLEX) PROGRAMS, 1985

Numbers and/or Descriptions of Teachers	Languages	Contacts
18 classroom teachers; 141 high school students; 33 adult volunteers; 1 principal	Spanish German French Latin Italian Japanese Portuguese Russian Hindi Korean	Gladys Lipton Coordinator, Foreign Languages and ESOL Anne Arundel County Public Schools 2644 Riva Road Annapolis, MD 21401 (301) 224-5424
Volunteers fluent in Spanish and English; participate in workshop to learn teaching techniques and how to use manual	Spanish	Linda Wood Program Consultant ADDitions School Volunteer Program Orange County Public Schools 410 Woods Avenue Orlando, FL 32805 (305) 422-5817
Regular classroom teachers teach FLEX classes; some have only limited knowledge of foreign language and learn language along with students with aid of audiotapes that accompany material	Spanish German French	Walter H. Bartz Foreign Language Educational Consultant Department of Education Division of Curriculum Room 229, State House Indianapolis, IN 46204 (317) 927-0111

About the Author

Linda Schinke-Llano (Ph.D., Northwestern University) teaches in the Linguistics Department of Northwestern University, where her responsibilities include directing the applied linguistics M.A. program, supervising teaching assistants, and teaching courses in sociolinguistics, second language acquisition, and bilingualism. Currently a member of the Editorial Advisory Board of the *TESOL Quarterly* and President of Illinois TESOL/BE, she has presented papers at TESOL, ACTFL, and NABE conferences. Her publications include research articles on second language acquisition, as well as numerous ESL materials--among them the *Everyday American English Dictionary* (with Richard Spears).

LANGUAGE IN EDUCATION: Theory and Practice

The Language in Education series is a collection of state-of-the-art papers, topical discussions, practical guides for classroom teachers, and selected bibliographies that has become a staple to language learning and teaching professionals. The monographs are prepared under the auspices of the ERIC Clearinghouse on Languages and Linguistics. They are then published by Harcourt Brace Jovanovich International and distributed worldwide.

Following are titles of particular interest to the foreign language audience. All orders should be sent to HBJ International, Orlando, FL 32887.

ACTFL 79. Abstracts of Presented Papers. 1980. (ED 183 031)

Assessing Study Abroad Programs for Secondary School Students, by Helene Z. Loew. 1980. (ED 193 974)

Children's Second Language Learning, by Barry McLaughlin. 1982. (ED 217 701)

Chinese Language Study in American Higher Education: State of the Art, by Peter Eddy, James Wrenn, and Sophia Behrens. 1980. (ED 195 166)

Code Switching and the Classroom Teacher, by Guadalupe Valdes-Fallis. 1978. (ED 153 506)

Computers and ESL, by David H. Wyatt. 1984. (ED 246 694)

Creative Activities for the Second Language Classroom, by Diane W. Birckbichler. 1982. (ED 217 702)

Discourse Analysis and Second Language Teaching, by Claire J. Kramsch. 1981. (ED 208 675)

Error Correction Techniques for the FL Classroom, by Joel C. Walz. 1982. (ED 217 704)

Evaluating a Second Language Program, by Gilbert A. Jarvis and Shirley J. Adams. 1979. (ED 176 589)

Foreign Languages, English as a Second/Foreign Language, and the U.S. Multinational Corporation, by Marianne Inman. 1979. (ED 179 089)

Functional-Notional Concepts: Adapting the FL Textbook, by Gail Guntermann and June K. Phillips. 1982. (ED 217 698)

Games and Simulations in the Foreign Language Classroom, by Alice C. Omaggio. 1979. (ED 177 877)

A Guide to Language Camps in the U.S.: 2, by Lois Vines. 1983. (ED 226 603)

Helping Learners Succeed: Activities for the Foreign Language Classroom, by Alice C. Omaggio. 1981. (ED 208 674)

The High School Goes Abroad: International Homestay Exchange Programs, by Phyllis J. Dragonas. 1983. (ED 233 591)

Intensive Foreign Language Courses, by David P. Benseler and Renate A. Schulz. 1979. (ED 176 587)

New Perspectives on Teaching Vocabulary, by Howard H. Keller. 1978. (ED 157 406)

The Older Foreign Language Learner: A Challenge for Colleges and Universities, by Elizabeth G. Joiner. 1981.. (ED 208 672)

Personality and Second Language Learning, by Virginia D. Hodge. 1978. (ED 157 408)

PR Prototypes: A Guidebook for Promoting Foreign Language Study to the Public, by Rosanne G. Royer et al. 1981. (ED 208 678)

Proficiency-Oriented Classroom Testing, by Alice C. Omaggio. 1983. (ED 233 589)

Reading a Second Language, by G. Truett Cates and
Janet K. Swaffar. 1979. (ED 176 588)

Sentence Combining in Second Language Instruction,
by Thomas Cooper et al. 1980. (ED 195 167)

*Teaching a Second Language: A Guide for the Student
Teacher*, by Constance K. Knop. 1980. (ED 195 165)

Teaching Culture: Strategies and Techniques, by
Robert C. Lafayette. 1978. (ED 157 407)

*Teaching French as a Multicultural Language: The
French-Speaking World Outside of Europe*, by John D.
Ogden. 1981. (ED 208 677)

*Teaching the Metric System in the Foreign Language
Classroom*, by Bette Le Feber Stevens. 1980.
(ED 195 168)

Teaching Writing in the Foreign Language Curriculum,
by Claire Gaudiani. 1982. (ED 209 961)

*Testing Oral Communication in the Foreign Language
Classroom*, by Walter H. Bartz. 1979. (ED 176 590)

Training Translators and Conference Interpreters, by
Wilhelm K. Weber. 1984. (ED 246 696)

Using Computers in Teaching Foreign Languages, by
Geoffrey R. Hope, Heimy F. Taylor, and James P.
Pusack. 1984. (ED 246 695)